Aging With Grace

✞

Reflections That Revive Women

Stephannie E. R. Solomon

authorHOUSE®

AuthorHouse™
1663 Liberty Drive
Bloomington, IN 47403
www.authorhouse.com
Phone: 1-800-839-8640

Published by AuthorHouse 11/28/2012

ISBN: 978-1-4772-8505-3 (sc)
ISBN: 978-1-4772-8504-6 (e)

Library of Congress Control Number: 2012920422
Any people depicted in stock imagery provided by Thinkstock are models,
and such images are being used for illustrative purposes only.
Certain stock imagery © Thinkstock.

This book is printed on acid-free paper.

All scripture footnotes are from the New International, Amplified, Message,
King James, Contemporary English Version and New Century Versions.

Other Solo Works By The Author

Conversations With The King
Living With The King

Contributed To:

Sister To Sister:Devotions For and From African
American Women
&
Sister Strength

Connect With The Author

https://twitter.com/StephannieBooks

http://www.blogtalkradio.com/stephanniesolomon

Conversations With The King Ministries, Inc. Facebook

http://www.stephanniesolomon.com

&

Conversations With The King Ministries, Inc.
P.O. Box 44444
Nottingham, MD 21236
410.661.5902

Contents

Dedication .xi

Preface. xv

Forever 20 Something 1

How Big Girls Roll 15

Taking Off The Weight 35

Winning Women 55

The Art Of Silence. 65

Let's Talk About Sex 77

I Declare 109

Super Models 123

He's Just That In To You. 151

The Sanctified Stripper 163

Dedication

Aging With Grace *is dedicated to one of my top fans and consistent encouragers, my daughter, Sierra Simone. Now a woman, continue to grow strong and wise in the Lord's grace my princess. Mommy will always love you.*

*But **grow in** the **grace** and knowledge of our Lord and Savior Jesus Christ. To him be glory both now and forever! Amen.*

2 Peter 3:18
The New International Version

Preface

I was 55 years old during the writing of and photo shoot for *Aging With Grace*. The time had come to dare to share what many Christian women discuss privately and want addressed publically. We are witnessing defeat in the lives of our girls, female teens, young and older women to seductive competitors of Christ on a mammoth scale. I know that it has only been by the *grace of God* that I and many other women have not been destroyed by the same deceptive tactics. It is my prayer that the Lord use this book to challenge, confront, convict and convert female readers for the cause of Christ Jesus.

Through a Christian woman's vision and voice, *Aging With Grace* works to assist in the revival of the feminine spirit. It will move girls and women forward in Christ Jesus. Each reflection offers females of faith nuggets of wisdom that set in motion a desire and plan of action to live life to its fullest in Christ. The chapters are intentionally provocative and stem from years of conversations, personal experiences and observations of the unique dynamics of church girls and Christian women. Like my previous books, the approach to this read is disciple-centric and the tone conversational. Foundational scriptures are highly peppered throughout the book. Each chapter culminates with end notes and a guide which allows readers to be reflective and engage with the author. By design the preface is meant to be brief so that you, the reader, can dive right in and be blessed. Enjoy and grow in the Grace of God!

Stephannie E. R. Solomon

Forever 20 Something

✟

And now here's what I want you to do: Tell the truth, the whole truth, when you speak. Do the right thing by one another, both personally and in your courts. (MSG)
Zechariah 8:16

Grace To Be You

Growing to become the authentic you can be a challenge, especially when your ego is vying for all of the attention. Yet, real living comes in the freedom to tell truths that ultimately transform our thinking and behaviors to godliness. This can be burdensome, especially living within a culture that defies truths about aging. So many women have been and still are held hostage to this matter of growing older. Now is the time to own who you are as well as the you who you are becoming. Owning the incredible, wonderful and unique you, is admitting your age without disgrace. It is by the grace of the Almighty God our Father that we are alive today. It is by His grace that we stand.[1] The Lord has allowed us to reach this stage of life; where we are today. Ladies this is God's grace. We did nothing to earn it, but our heavenly Father through Christ Jesus has given us opportunity upon opportunity to get it together in Him. Herein is the Lord's favor towards us; giving us what we do not deserve.

Aging Is A Part Of Life

As we live with the grace of God upon us, there should not be any embarrassment, fear or sadness about getting older. The grace of God covers us at any age.[2] The Lord says "Even when you are old, I will be the same. Even when your hair has turned gray, I will take care of you. I made you and will take care of you. I will carry you and save you". There should be a healthy embrace of aging especially in the Lord. How we embrace aging works to define us. It is God's grace that covers our stupidity, stubbornness and all sins during this miraculous process called growth. Thus, stand proudly in this wonderful gift of the Lord. Growing physically, emotionally, intellectually, and spiritually is the intention of our God. This is aging. The question for another day is, are you aging in all four areas? It is possible to live stunted in one or more of these areas.

Aging is a part of life; own it. It is amazing how as little girls many women tried on their mother's clothes, shoes and make up to appear older. They wanted to get a glimpse of what they might look like as an adult. Countless girls and teens have attempted to impress and even fool others through their choice of attire, strut, vices and speech. Then, at some point when these girls became women, they switched gears. They decided to attempt to return to those younger days through deceptions and alterations. The reasons vary from woman to woman. For some women it might have been stretch marks, unwelcomed weight gain, cracking of bones, graying and thinning hair, sagging breasts, lack of attention, bags under the eyes, wrinkles and freckles on the skin, loneliness, too much responsibility at home and/or work and this is where you fill in the blank_____. Whatever the stimulus, there are women who have decided to continue sharing a popular old wives' tale that declares that women should not reveal their age. Through light hearted jokes and other deflective means millions of women expose their poor perceptions about the aging journey. Focusing on the numbers matter more to some rather than praising God for His grace through the years. Despite the varied and often warped views on growing older, aging in the Lord actually has benefits.[3] There is a favorable appeal afforded to women who embrace this fact of life. They continue to be fresh and flourish at every phase of life.

Nothing But A Number

Modern society imparts that turning 30 years old is a point of dread. Suddenly, it's time to reflect when actually reflection should be a daily way of life for the Child of God. Reaching the age of 40 is over the hill; which suggest that you are past your prime or you are unable to function as you used to. The world offers ridiculous advice to us. After 40 we still have hills to climb, but as Women of God we look up to the hills knowing that our help will always come from the Lord God Almighty. The 40 to 50 year old range is not a time of crisis etched in stone. Crisis can happen at any time. It has no age preference. Rather than speak gloom over the aging process, we have to speak grace. At every stage, childhood, youth, teenage, young adult, senior; however, we choose to label our aging phase, the likelihood of troubles exists.

As Women of God, we have the hope in knowing that the Lord is able to keep us at any age. We are sustained by His grace and His grace is truly more than enough.[4] God's grace is active in your life and in mine. Speaking on the inevitable process of aging should not be a sore spot. Rather than shun the question or deflect by cracking a joke or getting angry, maximize the moment by staying on the true course. Spill the beans and openly give God the glory for where He has brought you. More often than not, you will see that most people are surprised because the grace of God has preserved you. Let's get real with this age old fear and lore about hiding our age. With grace, confront perpetuated ignorance and inferiorities.[5] Decide to defy aging phobias and declare, especially to the young among us just how old you really are. In an age where children entering adulthood are heavier than they have ever been at any time in human history, many look older than they actually are. Announcing that you and I are aging gracefully can be the witness on self-care and the keeping power of God that many young people need to hear.

Don't Hold Back

Some men have been taught never to ask a woman how old she is. In this day of identity theft, the down low lifestyle and other means of deception and dysfunction, men and women need to ask more questions of others on the front end. The consequences of not asking can be hazardous to our health, finances, families and more on the back end. Women traditionally, tend not to ask many questions of their husbands, fathers, male doctors and leaders in fear of being labeled a nag, highly opinionated or an "itch". Enough already! Women of God shake things up and shift gears. This age old practice of "if you ask I won't tell my age" is ridiculous. Where did this foolishness originate? One thing is for sure, the response to lie is built on personal fears and low self-image. There is no joke that can cover this madness.

Over the years I have established many healthy relationships with children and young adults. At some point in our conversations, especially around my birthday, the question of my age has risen. Being a mathematics educator I give some facts for them to set up a basic "algebraic" equation to solve. The current year is 2012 and the year of my birth was 1957.

$$1957 + s = 2012$$
$$1957 - 1957 + s = 2012 - 1957$$
$$s = 55 \text{ yrs. old}$$
$$\text{Check: } 1957 + 55 = 2012$$
$$2012 = 2012$$

The feedback is hilarious and actually strengthens our bond. They see that I will not lie to them. Young people are always watching us older ones to see if we have integrity in all things. Sometimes they are waiting to catch us living out double standards; deceptions. Something that may be seen as a little white lie is still a lie. Many women have no idea that they are counted as untrustworthy to those around them by deflecting from a simple truth. Really, if you lie about one thing, you are likely to lie about other things. When people see that you are uninhibited about ignorant cultural lore, they tend to come to you for advice in which they are ready to listen. They gain respect for you and what you have to say. Holding back on telling your age closes the doors of trust, integrity, accountability and credibility. I talk more about these agents of witnessing in Living With The King.[6] Certainly many women's flaky responses have perpetuated a custom that highlights their low self-esteem rather than high regard.

Game Changers

Accepting our age does not mean forgoing exercise, healthy diets, and even the wealth of beauty options for our hair, nails, breasts and other body parts. I believe in finding and going forward in what enhances our outer appearance. Truly work what works for you. However, every fad, trend or option does not work for everyone. Certainly as a Christian we do not embrace all options, exchange the truth about God for a lie or encourage and affirm alternate lifestyles even when man made laws approve of them.[7] Human law or ways are not always suitable for the purposes that God has in mind. If the revived you is twenty pounds lighter or heavier and you look stunning, own it. So be it if you shave your head bald or nearly bald. Work what you have. If you are feeling a new look with a weave, full lace wig, natural hair or a track or two, go for it. Rock the hairstyle of choice so that it adds to a graciously beautiful you.

You and I are still becoming in the Lord; therefore, rules that the world has set for us will be broken and its hope for our failures shall be deferred. Be courageous then and live against popular misguided opinions concerning you. Quit chasing the next thing that promises to make you forever 21, 25, 29 or 20 something. Break ranks from those who would have you continually live choosing what they think you ought to do and look like. I am not dismissing godly or sincere counsel, but owning warped opinions in regard to our lives is not an option. We are who the Lord says we are. It is His report that we should believe and receive throughout our journey, none other.

The world is running a game with its view and rules on aging. It detests godly maturity and has always sought alternatives to godly living. Complimenting, promoting, glorifying people who choose to model ungodly living is a specialty of the world. The world exchanges truth about God for a lie.[8] Women of Faith must choose daily to live by a different paradigm. Our model of exemplary living is Jesus Christ. His standards declare that we are fearfully and wonderfully made.[9] We are the salt of the earth which makes us game changers not game players.[10] Through the leading of the Lord Jesus Christ, we are to set it off and change the plans of the world's play book. Choosing to conform to the world's view and game is not what we are called and chosen by God to do.[11]

Christian women are in the world, yet like Christ, we are not of it.[12] We are of God.[13] He is Truth while Satan and the world are devoid of truth.[14] Since we are of God and He is Truth, then we too must reflect truth. With dignity, poise, elegance, femininity and class we can grow in the Lord and in the power of His might. In truth we shall celebrate where we are, for age is a stage of human life ordained by God. We will not remain at any one stage forever. We need the grace of God over us, every step and stage of our journey. Aging with grace will not keep us forever in our twenties, but with God's grace we will mature beautifully in Him.

Reflection

Prayer: Heavenly Father your will be done in my life. After reading "Forever 20 Something", I understand now that…

I am beautiful and lovely at age 46. I am confident in myself sometimes. But when I think about how much you love me I snap out of it. Because I am fearfully and wonderfully made.

Write a word that comes to mind when you reflect on the sub-topics of this chapter.

Grace To Be You	*and shared*
Aging Is A Part Of Life	*so live*
Nothing But A Number	*age*
Don't Hold Back	*Nothing*
Game Changers	*change of life*

How does the foundational scripture relate to this chapter?

[And now here's what I want you to do: Tell the truth, the whole truth, when you speak. Do the right thing by one another, both personally and in your courts, Zechariah 8:16]

Be honest with yourself and with others.

Some individuals are chasing the next model of a particular car, electronic device, etc. for various reasons. What are you chasing after? Expound.

to do what is right. I'm tired of committing the same sin over and over again.

Do you think that there is anything in life worth chasing? Expound.

Yes!

What myths about aging do you plan to dismiss or live to denounce?

Not telling your age

How do you plan to accomplish this?

I will tell my age to any-
one. Because God has
allowed me to be the age
I am now. Not many have
and the ones who are my age
look 10 x more older.
Thank You Lord

Share your comments and tweets on how the chapter "Forever 20 Something" blessed you on:

http://www.blogtalkradio.com/stephanniesolomon
https://twitter.com/StephannieBooks
Facebook/Conversations With The King Ministries

Chapter Endnotes

1. 1 Peter 5:12b I wrote to encourage you and to tell you that this is the true grace of God. Stand strong in that grace. (NCV)

2. Isaiah 46:4 Even when you are old, I will be the same. Even when your hair has turned gray, I will take care of you. I made you and will take care of you. I will carry you and save you. (NCV)

3. Psalm 92:14 [Growing in grace] they shall still bring forth fruit in old age; they shall be full of sap [of spiritual vitality] and [rich in the] verdure [of trust, love, and contentment]. (AMP)

4. 2 Corinthians 12:9a Three times I did that, and then he told me, My grace is enough; it's all you need. (MSG)

5. Johnson, Gregory. *The Kingdom According To Jesus.* North Charleston, South Carolina.:CreateSpace, 2012.

6. Stephannie Solomon. *Living With The King: Hallmarks Of Godly Servants.* Bloomington, Indiana, AuthorHouse, 2010, p. 110-114.

7. 1 Corinthians 6:12 and 1 Corinthians 10:23 All things are lawful unto me, but all things are not expedient: all things are lawful for me, but I will not be brought under the power of any (but all things edify not) (KJV)

8. Romans 1:25 They exchanged the truth about God for a lie. (NIV)

9. Psalm 139:14 I praise you because I am fearfully and wonderfully made; your works are wonderful, I know that full well. (NIV)

10. Matthew 5:13 You are the salt of the earth, but if salt has lost its taste (its strength, its quality), how can its saltiness be restored? It is not good for anything any longer but to be thrown out and trodden underfoot by men.(NIV)

11. Romans 12:2 And be not conformed to this world: but be ye transformed by the renewing of your mind, that ye may prove what is that good, and acceptable, and perfect, will of God. (KJV)

12. John 17:16 They are not of the world (worldly, belonging to the world), [just] as I am not of the world. (AMP)

13. 1 John 5:19 We know [positively] that we are of God, and the whole world [around us] is under the power of the evil one. (AMP)

14. John 14:6 Jesus said, "I am the Road, also the Truth, also the Life. No one gets to the Father apart from me. (MSG)

How Big Girls Roll

✟

Roll your works upon the Lord [commit and trust them wholly to Him; He will cause your thoughts to become agreeable to His will, and] so shall your plans be established and succeed. (AMP)
Proverbs 16:3

Big Is Better

Do what you do, express your swag, and know that big girls in Christ roll differently than other women. In no way am I targeting tall or weighty women in the physical realm or sense. However, this message is aimed at the great and mighty women growing in grace in God's Kingdom. They are authentic power houses and game changers in Jesus Christ. They are grown women with a mind-set to honor the Lord as He sees fit so He uses them to change the way typical situations develop. These remarkable ladies may lose something as they follow Christ. A decision moment that glorifies God may cost them much, but they strut on knowing that God's grace is sufficient. Yes, His grace is sufficient not ours.[1] They see themselves as servants and the Lord as Master without issue. Words like submission, obedience, Master, servant and trust do not make them cringe. They are comfortable in the skin that they are in and serve the Lord with gladness. These women are not ashamed of the grace of God and certainly not the gospel of Jesus Christ.

There is a distinct line of demarcation that separates big girls who are of the world from big girls who are in the world, but not of it. The world and haters will disagree with the godly standards and expectations of God's big girls, but they cannot deny what is witnessed. On lookers will take notice of spiritually mature women living out of their convictions. They see big girls who truly care that their character is being developed by God alone. They roll or live large in the Lord.

Yes, big girls in Jesus roll differently. They know that their life is validated by their total dependence on the Lord. The foundational scripture of this chapter, Proverbs 16:3, comes from the Amplified translation. It uses the word "roll" which means to commit or cast your works onto the Lord. God declares that our plans will be established and that we shall succeed if we roll our mission, our project, that assignment onto Him. The scripture further explains that as you and I commit our works wholly to the Lord, our thoughts become influenced by Him. They become agreeable to His will for us, aligned to what He knows is best.

As big girls grow in Christ, they know that by continually casting their cares onto Him they expose their confidence in the one who tells His disciples to take His yoke and learn from Him. These Women of God have learned that the Lord will perfect, bring to an end, that which concerns them. These disciples have discovered that it is just a matter of time that trouble will subside and be made beautiful by the Lord since God makes all things beautiful in its time.[2] Living big in God has benefits. Truly, big is better. This better way to live is an ongoing process that reveals changes in behaviors and attitudes that ultimately glorify God. These godly shifts are not normal in the world in which we live. Our reform should be normal, but in a world that is an enemy to God, it will be unusual. In many instances how we choose to think is considered abnormal. Those who are in the world, will ask, "Who does that"? We may be called mavericks, leaders, game changers, lone wolves and so on, but one thing is true, being a big girl makes us peculiar. We are holy to God who has chosen us out of all of the people on the earth to be different than the world's view.[3] Living as a big woman makes us about God's big business. We are not about the petty because we have "big fish to fry". Thus, our lifestyle is odd to the world and those around us.

Wise As A Snake

The features of big girls are phenomenal. One particular distinction is adaptability. Using what the good Lord has given them, big girls adjust to the condition, environment or situation at hand and make "it" work for them rather than have the situation run, rule and ruin them. They roll with the punches by rethinking, reworking, resolving, resting, relinquishing, reinventing or reconciling if need be. Opposition and frustration are not permitted to thwart the modifications needed for their survival and successes.

Adapting new and different ideas makes big girls stand out from the crowd. They are non-conformists who, through Christ Jesus, transform the way that something is done, thought or made. They possess radical faith in the face of stubborn scourges. Believing every word that proceeds out of the mouth of the Lord is how they roll, what they do habitually.[4] Trusting God like this can be risky business, but adapting His word to one's life has great rewards. Remember this world is an enemy to God and surely not a friend to grace. Thus, we need not just any word, but the Word of God to save and sustain us.

One of many scriptures that transforms and transports big girls is Matthew 10:16. Here Jesus says, "Listen, I am sending you out like sheep among wolves. So be as clever as snakes and as innocent as doves." Look at Jesus using a snake as a point of reference for his servants to learn from. Snakes are one of the most feared creatures on earth. Yet, they have adapted to multiple climates; they are found almost everywhere. Their habitats are in mountains, deserts, in the sea, rivers, lakes, even in the Arctic. Snakes have developed adaptations to a wide variety of environments. They have learned to survive in the desert by attaining a level of coolness; some hibernate during the fall and winter. These creatures can swim, climb, lie on rocks in the sun and hide near small fires for warmth. Snakes burrow under the earth to get cool and to find food. Some are known to glide through the air which gives the appearance of flying. Many can spring forward so that it appears as though they are jumping and leaping. Scientists have discovered that many snakes have evolved physically to meet and master the demands of their habitat. They know how to wait, watch and weather challenging conditions. Take note of this creature who has taken necessary measures to survive thousands of years. Are we not more than a snake?

Interestingly, the Lord does not reference cave men, birds or other creatures, but the crafty snake to show resourcefulness and adaptability. Like the snake, big girls in Christ also survive the harsh conditions of this world. We forge ahead, confront and conquer the challenges of life. Will decisions always be easy and without risks? No. Will there be costs? Yes. Will there be losses incurred? It is very possible. Yet, in all "these things" we are more than conquers.[5] None of "these things" move us.[6] Let the "these things" in life be anything that is a hindrance to our survival in Christ Jesus. We too can endure seasons of hardships and win. We can do this because first, we love the Lord and secondly, because we believe that no good thing will be withheld from us due to our blameless walk.[7]

There are other facets to the Lord's big girl. However, there is one that is most worthy of mention; she is humble. God's big girls do not wait to be humbled by life's circumstances; they humble themselves.[8] Choosing to live God's way will make anyone a humble servant. It is written that humility comes before honor.[9] So many sisters want honor, but fail to see the link and significance of being a humble soul. God wants us to be honored, but having honor does not mean making a monument of oneself. Jesus is the Good Shepherd and we are the sheep of His pasture, it is God who has made us and not we ourselves. The Lord is the Vine and we are the branches. As much as we want to perceive that we are the boss, captain of our fate, or the reason for being here; we are not our own.[10] Women of God we have been bought with a price; purchased of God. Now let the redeemed of the Lord say so and become humbled.

Humble Pie

Humility is a virtue.[11] It is not something that you or I declare; it is the essence of who we are. If we have to say that we are humble, there is reason to believe that we are anything but humble. False humility my sister will not cut it. I like how Charles Haddon Spurgeon penned it in one of his sermons; "Humility is a thing which must be genuine; the imitation of it is the nearest thing in the world to pride."[12] So be careful not to misinterpret truths or make yourself and your accomplishments little adored gods. Have faith in God.[13] Learn of Him, lean on and always look and listen to Him. These action principles will develop the needed, strong and genuine trait of humility. The mathematics educator in me wants you to recall these as L^4 (L to the fourth power). Learning, leaning, looking and listening help us discover God's power at work in us. Neglect and denial of these essentials will surely lead to pride. Where self-aggrandizement and any form of pride abide, personal disaster is certainly very near for the disciple.[14] Pride is the complete opposite of humility and it is not always easily recognized in us by us. Where it resides, destruction is sure to follow.[15] It is one of several things that God reveals his distaste for.[16]

Humility can be forced upon us often after embarrassing conditions have evolved due to our pride and over confidence. Self-sufficiency should not be the lifestyle of the Christian, but rather total sufficiency in Christ.[17] The Lord will permit our downfall to take place sometimes so that we see that we have thought more highly of ourselves than of Him.[18] There are times when the Lord sets into motion preventive measures such as humble beginnings or a season of travail. It is a prescription for humility. The apostle Paul sought the

Lord through prayer three times to remove something in his life that was bothersome. The Lord's response to Paul was that His grace was enough for the situation. Paul realized that this particular struggle kept him humbled; it prevented conceit.[19] Yes, our Sovereign Lord permits and prevents to prepare us for the bounty ahead. The bounty can be great gifting, an anointing to marvel over and/or physical wealth. Whatever the event the Lord engineers; He knows how to kill pride, conceit, piousness, selfishness and self-righteousness. His weapon of choice is often humility. It is a virtue that we blossom through. My dear sister humility or humble pie has been prepared for you and I. Eat it and grow strong in the Lord and in the power of His might.

Women of God are new creatures in Christ, so we must accept the challenge to grow up in Him. A turning point will cause us to do just that, become Abba's big girl. Choosing to remain as His little girl will stunt our spiritual growth. We can grow and do it with grace. Embrace all that it takes to grow and become great in His sight and in the presence of others. Acknowledge His unmerited favor that has been and remains over you. Recognize the strong and godly character that He has given you. *Become a Big Girl who can walk with grace and grit simultaneously.* God's grace is enough. Be strong in the Lord and in the power of His might. Do not give your time, energy, intellect, heart and vigor to things that are irrelevant. They simply do not matter. Rather support and invest in the things of God that matter much. People need to see and are waiting to see someone who is successful with the Lord's blessings and burdens. Be that person, that woman who models confidence in Jesus. Show the world how God's big girls roll.

High Maintenance

Depending on whom you ask the definition of a high maintenance woman varies. Many composed lists range from must have high end purchases to being emotionally needy. From reading and listening to conversations on this subject, from both males and females, I have concluded that this is a male driven issue because the vastness of publically shared information on this topic is coming from men. Many men are having a problem with the packaging of some women. I get that many of them find materialistic women distasteful. I fully understand their discomfort dating and being married to a self-absorbed woman. To be uncomfortable in a relationship with someone who only sees herself as the focal point of attention is not a good sign. The male driven blogs, books and beliefs are pure negative. However, like everything, there is always another perspective.

I have become concerned that in this age of labeling, subtle bullying, cookie-cutter marketing, illicit imaging and name calling desperate women are allowing this term to influence their personal expectations as well as what to expect in a date and potential mate. Consider that a woman lives by God's declarations for her life. She declares Psalm 139:14 over herself, that she is fearfully and wonderfully made. She uses scripture to declare also that her body is the temple of the Holy Spirit. She speaks affirmations over herself, knowing that in order for an affirmation to truly be affirming it must be true. So she looks for Truth which is the Word of God. This confidence and reliance on the Lord can make a prospective mate uncomfortable.

When a woman loves the Lord enough to trust Him at His every word, which includes keeping her, then the man should be even more excited about who he has in his presence. If God's word is supreme in her life, more than likely, she will respect, honor, appreciate and love on the man that the Lord has given her. She should not have a problem doing what the Words of God direct her to do in all areas of her life. No man should be intimidated with a woman who obediently puts the Lord first. Surely he will get good loving and attention from such a yielded vessel. In addition, when the woman gets out of order, because she is a Woman of God, he can believe that she will come to her senses because of the Lord's convicting power over her heart, mind and spirit. Now I am a realist. It is what it is. As much as I believe that the Lord can do anything, there are times when people of God walk away from the things of God.[20] They are not forced to turn from the Lord. They voluntarily separate themselves from what the Lord requires of them for reasons that are not of God.[21] God does not have us turn from Him. If there is any turning, it is to turn to Him. People of God do not always uphold righteousness and do choose sin over sanctity. It happens.

There is a difference between the divas, prima donnas, gold-diggers, foo-foo girls and a kept woman. What they have in common is an expectation to be kept or maintained in high regard. The difference is that the kept woman does not see herself as the center of all attention, rather Christ is her center. The line of demarcation is that the kept woman of God relies on Him to provide for her needs, while giving to Him her best of worship, praise, thanksgiving and service. She will be cared for totally because God is her reward.[22] Her expectation is in Him, not herself or anyone else.[23] Even if the Lord chooses to use a person to bless her, she is aware that this is of the Lord. It is His doing and is a marvelous thing.[24] God rewards her for her diligence, obedience and faithfulness to Him. He covers her with godliness. According to 1Timothy 6:6 she has much. Godliness with satisfaction in Jesus Christ is wealth. Little wonder those without a discerning eye think that some of God's Women require much. He makes us look great and confident even when we are unsure of tomorrow. For the insecure man with an agenda to belittle women, these features can be threatening.

God's Woman should never apologize for expecting that which is good from the Lord, especially if she is more than a church goer. She ought to expect great things from the Great God as she does her part to live in Him. Anyone who takes liberty to tell us to expect subpar and settle for less is not speaking the language of Christ. Our relationship with Him is one of give and take. God gives so much to us. We receive His blessings. Since we are in relationship with Him, we too give to Him. We give back our funds, our marriage, our children, our mind and so much more. He takes these things and works wonders through them in our lives. We are givers. Being highly maintained in Christ, we have learned that it is better to give than to receive, for our blessing comes from giving.[25] Also, giving to God with a cheerful heart counts for much, for this is the attitude that pleases Him.[26] Herein, we see that Women of God, God's Kept Women who are highly maintained by Him, stand out from the rest.

So many people have an opinion on something. Loving and trusting the Lord is a virtue. However, if a man or anyone sees these attributes as poor qualities, truly they have a God problem. Having a God problem will trickle down to individuals having a problem with His people. This should not dismay or sway God's woman, for He still will take care of His own.[27] High maintenance in Christ Jesus should not scare a single man desiring to approach God's single ladies. Christ is guiding her with His high standards to live by and they should not disappear because someone is in disagreement to His ways. She is striving to become virtuous and a woman of holy standards. Thus, ladies must do more than thinking about raising personal standards. When the Lord's standards are adopted, personal standards will align and ascend, for God lifts standards that overtake our enemies, not us (Isaiah 59:19). Raising our standards without Christ is fruitless. In and of ourselves we do not know what is good, so how can we live assured that we are living rightly before God? Only God is good and knows what is considered good.[28] Our standard is our way and our ways always lead to failure and some form of death (Proverbs 14:12 and Proverbs 16:25). Moreover, history and our track record prove that our standards may please us, but they never work to please the Lord.

Women of Worth, it is healthy to love you without being conceited and self-absorbed. It is also fine to have an expectation of sharing your love of self with a man who appreciates you, rather than looking for a man to complete your self-love deficit. There are people who will hate the fact that you love you. It is difficult to control a girl or woman who knows of the value and worth that the Lord has deposited in her. If someone has an issue with you loving and respecting your body, mind and spirit, they obviously had a malicious agenda in mind for you which include control and manipulation. We are to be controlled only by the Holy Spirit who guides us into loving on Him and then loving on ourselves so that we can love on others.

Everyone is not happy to witness self-confidence and self-respect with the absence of narcissism. Again, that is there problem that we should not embrace. Neither should we allow ourselves to feel guilty for disagreeing with such disapproval of what the Lord has deposited within His female vessels. When the enemies of Christ speak through people and circumstances, and they will, know that the Spirit of the Lord will lift up a standard against them.[29] His standard will always surpass options and conquer that which contends with His plan. He is our keeper. He will maintain our sanity and so much more. Never apologize for being loved, cared for and supported by God. Question the motives of anyone who believes that Women of Worth are not deserving of God's affection towards them. In this, be careful not to think more highly of yourselves than you should, yet accept that He who is highly exalted has a plan of high maintenance for women who are highly esteemed, highly valued and highly favored by the High God.

Reflection

Prayer: Lord I want to be successful and at peace in you. While reading "How Big Girls Roll" I realized that...

_____
_____
_____
_____
_____
_____
_____

There are several scriptures noted within this chapter. Which one stands out to you and why?

_____
_____
_____
_____

When was the last time that Grace and Grit worked together to strengthen you?

_____
_____
_____
_____

Did your response give God the glory? Expound.

_____
_____
_____
_____
_____

How does the foundational scripture relate to this chapter?

[Roll your works upon the Lord [commit and trust them wholly to Him; He will cause your thoughts to become agreeable to His will, and] so shall your plans be established and succeed. Proverbs 16:3]

_____
_____
_____
_____
_____

Being labeled as a high maintenance woman has more of a negative connotation in the world than a positive one. What do you think women can do to change this perception?

_____
_____
_____
_____

How might men change their expectations about women who want respect, love and appreciation?

_____
_____
_____
_____

Would you want to be labeled as high maintenance? Why or why not?

_____
_____
_____
_____

The world uses sayings such as "follow your heart" and "my man completes me". As nice as these sound, how are they misleading for a girl and woman of God?

_____

_____

_____

_____

_____

_____

_____

_____

Share your comments and tweets on how the chapter "How Big Girls Roll" blessed you on:

https://twitter.com/StephannieBooks
http://www.blogtalkradio.com/stephanniesolomon
Facebook/Conversations With The King Ministries

Chapter Endnotes

1. 2 Corinthians 3:5 Not that we are sufficient of ourselves to think anything as of ourselves; but our sufficiency is of God. (KJV)

2. Ecclesiastes 3:11 God has given them a desire to know the future. He does everything just right and on time, but people can never completely understand what he is doing. (NCV)

3. Deuteronomy 14:2 For you are a holy people [set apart] to the Lord your God; and the Lord has chosen you to be a peculiar people to Himself, above all the nations on the earth. (AMP)

4. Matthew 4:4 Jesus answered, "It is written in the Scriptures, A person lives not on bread alone, but by everything God says. (NCV)

5. Romans 8:37 Yet amid all these things we are more than conquerors and gain a surpassing victory through Him Who loved us. (AMP)

6. Acts 20:24 But none of these things move me, neither count I my life dear unto myself, so that I might finish my course with joy, and the ministry, which I have received of the Lord Jesus, to testify the gospel of the grace of God. (KJV)

7. Psalm 84:11 For the Lord God is a Sun and Shield; the Lord bestows [present] grace and favor and [future] glory (honor, splendor, and heavenly bliss)! No good thing will He withhold from those who walk uprightly.(AMP)

8. James 4:10 Humble yourself in the Lord's presence and he will honor you. (NCV)

9. Proverbs 15:33 Wisdom's instruction is to fear the LORD, and humility comes before honor. (NIV)

10. 1 Corinthians 6:19 You should know that your body is a temple for the Holy Spirit who is in you. You have received the Holy Spirit from God. So you do not belong to yourselves. (NCV)

11. Micah 6:8 He has showed you, O man, what is good. And what does the Lord require of you but to do justly, and to love kindness and mercy, and to humble yourself and walk humbly with your God? (AMP)

12. Charles Haddon Spurgeon, *Pride and Humility*, August 17, 1856.

13. Mark 11:22 Jesus answered, Have faith in God. (NCV)

14. Proverbs 18:12 Before a downfall the heart is haughty, but humility comes before honor. (NIV)

15. Proverbs 16:18 Pride goeth before destruction, and an haughty spirit before a fall. (KJV)

16. Proverbs 6:16-19 Here are six things God hates, and one more that he loathes with a passion: eyes that are arrogant, a tongue that lies, hands that murder the innocent, a heart that hatches evil plots, feet that race down a wicked track, a mouth that lies under oath, a troublemaker in the family. (MSG)

17. 2 Corinthians 3:5a Not that we are sufficient of

ourselves to think anything as of ourselves; but our sufficiency is of God. (KJV)

18. Romans 12:3 [*Humble Service in the Body of Christ*] For by the grace given me I say to every one of you: Do not think of yourself more highly than you ought, but rather think of yourself with sober judgment, in accordance with the faith God has distributed to each of you. (AMP)

19. 2 Corinthians 12:7b-9 Therefore, in order to keep me from becoming conceited, I was given a thorn in my flesh, a messenger of Satan, to torment me. [8] Three times I pleaded with the Lord to take it away from me. [9] But he said to me, "My grace is sufficient for you, for my power is made perfect in weakness. " Therefore I will boast all the more gladly about my weaknesses, so that Christ's power may rest on me.(NIV)

20. Luke 9:59-62 He said to another man, "Follow me." But he replied, "Lord, first let me go and bury my father. Jesus said to him, "Let the dead bury their own dead, but you go and proclaim the kingdom of God. Still another said, "I will follow you, Lord; but first let me go back and say goodbye to my family." Jesus replied, "No one who puts a hand to the plow and looks back is fit for service in the kingdom of God.(NIV)

21. Stephannie Solomon. *Living With The King: Voluntary Separation.* Bloomington, Indiana, AuthorHouse, 2010, p. 131-134.

22. Genesis 15:1 After these things, the word of the Lord came to Abram in a vision, saying, Fear

not, Abram, I am your Shield, your abundant compensation, and your reward shall be exceedingly great. (AMP)

23. Psalm 62:5 My soul, wait thou only upon God; for my expectation is from him. (KJV)

24. Psalm 118:23 the LORD has done this, and it is marvelous in our eyes. (NIV)

25. Acts 20:35 I showed you in all things that you should work as I did and help the weak. I taught you to remember the words Jesus said: 'It is more blessed to give than to receive.' (NCV)

26. 2 Corinthians 9:7 Each of you should give what you have decided in your heart to give, not reluctantly or under compulsion, for God loves a cheerful giver. (NIV)

27. Isaiah 41:10 Fear thou not; for I am with thee: be not dismayed; for I am thy God: I will strengthen thee; yea, I will help thee; yea, I will uphold thee with the right hand of my righteousness. (KJV)

28. Luke 18:19 Jesus said to him, "Why do you call me good? Only God is good. (NCV)

29. Isaiah 59:19 So shall they fear the name of the LORD from the west, and his glory from the rising of the sun. When the enemy shall come in like a flood, the Spirit of the LORD shall lift up a standard against him. (KJV)

Taking Off The Weight

✝

Therefore we also, since we are surrounded by so great a cloud of witnesses, let us lay aside every weight, and the sin which so easily ensnares us, and let us run with endurance the race that is set before us. (NKJV)
Hebrews 12:1

We Are What We Eat

All have sinned and come short of the glory of God.[1] I know that some of us have gotten churchified and now speak Christianese, but we have sinned and the propensity to sin lies within each of us. Moreover, the Holy Spirit says that if we say that this is untrue, we are lying.[2] Saints do sin. Disciples of Jesus Christ do miss the mark. What should separate us from sinners who are not Children of God is that we have an advocate who is Jesus Christ. By His grace we get forgiven and cleansed of our sins as soon as we confess them to Him.[3] He desires that we live free; free from sin and the weights of life. Christ Jesus came to give us a full life, not always a full plate, but a full life in His name.[4]

Jesus said that it takes more than bread to keep us going. We need a steady intake of God's Word to truly live the good life.[5] There is no getting around this. The Word of God is alive.[6] God is alive, The Son of God is alive; thus, to consume and incorporate what they have to say will give us the best life ever. Ingesting and applying the Word of God to our lives is food for our souls. It is "difficult" to sin and/ or remain married to sin when the Word of God is hidden in our heart.[7] Notice I wrote difficult. Our Master Builder has given each of us free will and the best among us can choose unrighteousness over righteousness at any given moment. Even then the nutrients of God's Word will revive us when we ingest the scriptures regarding confession, repentance, forgiveness and restoration.

We fall short for the lack of proper eating. We are essentially what we eat and what we fail to eat. Like a diet for our physical bodies, our spiritual self needs nourishment. Many of you can attest to the fact that as soon as you decide to feed your physical body the right foods, you have withdrawal symptoms and cravings for the wrong foods which aim to sabotage or limit progress. Giving in to the body's protest only keeps the unneeded weight on. In like manner, the mind and body disapprove of spiritual food. The flesh, the old nature protests that which will make us healthy in every area of our being. Due to a myriad of reasons, many disciples choose to hold onto sin as well as weighty issues that hold up our progress. Thus, we live with weights that hinder us. Added to our weight issue is the fact that we now know what is right; that which we should do, but decide not to. Let me rephrase the last sentence. We now know that the Word of God, which is food for our souls, must be eaten regularly. Many of the Lord's people choose not to eat it. Scripture says that to know what is right and choose the contrary is sin.[8] Yet, it is the knowing and execution of the scriptures that free us from weights and sin.

Like many pleasure in life, food can be addictive. However, it is essential that we establish a habit of eating God's Word on a daily basis. When we taste His word we get hooked because we see just how good He is.[9] Consistent intake of God's Word does a body good. What a feast, what a fare. It is delightful to indulge in the eating of the words of our Savior.[10] They free the mind, save and revive our souls. Nothing compares to coming upon a Word from the Lord which causes our heart to leap. It strengthens us and gives hope that surpasses the moment of seemingly hopelessness. As we eat it, the amazing grace of God is revealed to us, for all of God's Word is life, liberty, light and love. Even if we swallow God's Word whole we will be happy.

There are so many benefits to eating the Word of the Lord. Amazingly, one cannot overeat and become sick from God's Word. We can be food addicts with God's Words and this is a good thing. Being a Word addict is pleasurable, fulfilling, our delight and desire. We become healthy and whole as we are consumed and influenced by it. Our steps are ordered as we are addicted and attached to the Words of God.[11] Disciples are disciplined by it. There is life in everything that comes from the mouth of the Lord. Our devotion to Him is rooted deep as we grow from the nutrients of His words. We become liberators and agents of godly change because what we have eaten is the Word of God .

Getting Fit

Without question we become unfit and undernourished warriors when we carry unnecessary weight and sin. There are many weights in life as well as sins that are not itemized in scripture. However, they all are categorized in scripture and are revealed to us by the Holy Spirit. Therefore, it is important that we know both the Word and Voice of God to identify our weights as well as our sin. Weights and sin are intangible, yet real. They hinder and entangle. Both thrive in disbelief. They reveal our belief system in regard to God and His Word. Neither work to lead us to the "abundant life" that is promised to every disciple of Jesus Christ. Women of God must recognize weights and turn them over to Christ. Herein, we are exercising our faith, belief and trust in God.

As our physical body requires continual exercise, so too does our spirit. We need to be physically and spiritually fit to serve the Lord with gladness. Being in shape is a reflection of the Word that we consume. However, being inconsistent and lax in our walk creates portholes for the Lord's enemy to attack us. We create chinks in our armor where Satan's darts can hit and harm us. It will be the continual use of the principles of God and weapons of God that will defeat all works of our enemies. Thus, exercising the inner woman is essential for triumphs, tests and temptations. Reading and applying the Word of God daily will tone our spiritual muscles and make us in tune to what is attempting to become a weight in our lives. Never ceasing to pray about and over anything is not an exercise in futility.[12] Daily intakes of fruit, veggies, protein and exercise are great for the body; however, regular prayer, fasting, thanksgiving, praise, worship and application of God's Word make us spiritually fit.

Lifting our weights does not make us strong. What makes us strong is casting the care or dropping the weights onto Christ.[13] Standing in His grace and in the liberty where He has made us free is empowering. This is exercising our faith and belief in Him. If we do not trust what the Lord says, we then cast doubt on our situation. Worry, anxiety, delusion and other nemeses are sure to soon follow. A negative belief system about what GOD is doing, not doing or permitting becomes a weight. This oppressive heaviness must be laid aside for our well-being and progress. If we choose not to lay aside the weight it can very well become a stronghold; a layered and fortified fortress. No good thing is intended to get in or break through, but I thank God for His grace that can penetrate any barrier and reach us. In His time and with tender loving care, the Lord is able to deliver us from weight gain.

Sis Got Issues

Many girls and women have become comfortable and familiar with their unwanted weight. Neediness, self-sabotage, anger, dysfunction, comparison, competition, low self-esteem, poor self-image, secrets, indecisiveness, combativeness, immaturity, insecurity, the need to control, abuses, are just a few weights common among the sisterhood. These and other weights are sometimes labeled as baggage. When these weights are not addressed properly they interfere with the normal healthy emotional and psychological growth course determined for a girl or woman and her relationships. As long as they are unidentified, isolated and ignored, they will run rampant in a sister's life becoming baggage carried into every relation she enters.

These weights and assortment of baggage are issues that must be confronted and shut down. Unfortunately, society's report card on helping and healing with female issues does not make the grade. Yes, some talk shows have good intentions with guests having medical backgrounds to addresses causes and effects of some of these weights, but as a whole we are not meeting success with healing and deliverance. Ladies we are our sister's keeper and we are missing this. Television shows and internet videos are reeling with footage of girls and women in brawls and aggressive confrontations with men and other women. Bad girl images are competing with dignity and grace. Society is capitalizing off of an underlying weight that needs to be put down or laid aside. Truly sisters helping sisters in the Lord can help make a dent in this chaos, not society.

Unfortunately, an aspect of the church, the Body of Christ, the Bride of Christ, whom I love, is also missing it. Conferences that have women-centric titles are not tilting the scales as they should either. So often many gatherings of this sort are more focused on the presenters than the attendees. Many women leave such assemblies just as wounded, worn out and weighted down as they were upon entry. Weekly, yearly get togethers sometimes do more harm than good. If all you gather for is to vent about being a victim and derive partnership in sympathy and sin, expect to remain over weight. Partaking in flaky prayers called intercession and prayers of witchcraft are leaving women more damaged and less knowledgeable about the saving grace of Jesus Christ.[14] I am an intercessor and one thing that rubs my spirit is a fake prayer labeled as intercessory prayer. Moreover, catchy titles and celebrities who are not servants of God may draw us to the function, but these things will not heal us. Sisters with issues are not made whole by fluff.

Subsequently, it seems so much easier for us to label a sister as having issues or being a piece of work rather than defining her as the Lord's handiwork.[15] We all should be willing to help sisters with issues, even if it is simply by modeling godliness before her. Even as we do our part to help, whether large or small, we must know that society and the sisterhood are not totally responsible for our loss of weighty baggage and issues. The choice to be free comes from within. Every woman must decide to stand in the liberty where Christ Jesus has made her free.[16] In many instances fear of what releasing the weight might entail supersedes faith; thus, the weight remains, solidifying itself in the disciple's life. Each weight encourages more weight gain. Trying to lose the weight becomes frustrating and seemingly impossible, but whatever is impossible with us is possible with God.[17] It is not the Lord's will that any of us perish and it is not His will that we live with heaviness of any sort for longer than we have to.[18] At His appointed time any weight can be lifted from our lives. Nothing is too hard for Him.[19] That said, let Him touch the weight.[20] Stop trying to heal one self. Yes, we know us better than others, but the Lord, our Maker, knows us better than we know ourselves. He is the Lord our Healer, who has sent His Word to heal our infirmities. He knows how the weight was accrued and has a plan to eradicate it.

Complex or simple, the way of the Lord is perfect.[21] He gives good instructions that are always meant to bless us never to harm us. God knows what He is doing. We are the ones who do not always know what the Lord is up to. We have to choose to believe that He will not lie nor abandon us. Trust in Him should allow us to do what He says; lay our weights aside. As long as we hold on to our weights we are immobile and bound in various realms. Yet, when we trust and believe the Lord we move forward in Him prospering along the way. We have taken Him at His word and are no longer bound emotionally, spiritually or psychologically. We are called to move forward so the weight has to be laid aside, out of our direction of movement.

There is an appointed time in all of our lives that the Lord has planned to release us from something. However, the Lord has also planned that there are moments in our lives that require us to release something and trust His grace with the results. Telling us to lay aside the weight is synonymous to releasing that which annoys, offends and often suppresses our joy. My dear sister, trust the Lord to do with it what He sees fit. Somehow, someway He will use the weight to work for your good.[22] At this juncture only signs and wonders are to be expected from The Great and Loving God. The weight loss will be great and the benefits of its absence significant. Do not doubt Him by leaning on your understanding.[23] There is no one who can take on our weight and use it to empower us like the Lord. Just imagine that which weighed us down is now used to uplift and even qualify us for an unseen mission that is intended to glorify the Lord. God is awesome. He removes the unwanted and uses it at the same time to do right by us. No one else can do this but Him.

Live And Let Die

For many women releasing a weight, letting egregious offenses go or dropping an issue sometimes can be easier said than done. Although prayerful for the removal of a particular weight, there are those who find it difficult to even imagine life without it. Laying a weight aside, giving it up or turning it over to the Lord can be a real challenge. Yet, choosing to maintain a spiritual weight reflects fear of moving forward into the unfamiliar; virgin territory. Whatever the excuse, reason or belief, facets of fear are underlying causes for keeping the weight on. To lay aside the weight means to start living again. It demonstrates the willingness to allow the Lord to rebuild us and our lives. Hence, in order to truly live the abundant life that Christ has promised His followers, we must intentionally drop something; allow it to die.

The death or release of something does not mean that all is lost; although some losses are necessary. All is not lost when the Lord tells us to release it, drop it, lay it aside or let something go. His Spirit will assure us of this fact by urging us to get moving forward, start working and even rework that which remains. There will be people who do not understand how we can walk away from a relationship, job, career, or a one in a life time offer. They cannot see or will not agree to what the Lord is doing in our life. Yet, we have to trust Him and continue strong as though we can see the God who no one can see.[24] If you and I struggle with letting something go or counting our losses, then we risk sabotaging future victories that have been planned just for us.

It is not uncommon to feel a sense of grief at the thought of leaving the familiar. In such times briefly mourn what the weight's absence represents. Notice that the mourning of the weight is brief. The Lord understands our need to mourn, but He has a time constraint on our mourning.[25] It is a short season. Notice what the Lord says to the prophet Samuel after the death of King Saul, "How long will you mourn for Saul, since I have rejected him as king over Israel? Fill your horn with oil and be on your way; I am sending you to Jesse of Bethlehem. I have chosen one of his sons to be king." This may seem insensitive, but this is the patient, loving God speaking. He has zero tolerance for extending the mourning session beyond what He has allowed. Samuel had different reasons for mourning so long, but the Lord needed to continue using him to judge Israel. Just as He had plans for Samuel, He has plans for us. Mourn and live. There are things that have to get done in the span of time ordained by God.

It is not always simple to get over hurts, but overcoming them is possible. The key to getting past them is taking the Lord at His word. Next, release the weight, your situation and burden to Him. Christ will do right by you Sis. He is true to His word. Mourn if you have to. Grieving brings out inner emotions that contributed to heaviness of the weight. It is ok and it is important. Trust Christ to handle every kind of emotion that is revealed. After dropping the weight, do not pick it up again by worrying and having anxiety over it.

Permit the weight to die and do not interfere with the dying process. Allow the hand of the Lord to make your weight disappear. Just as the Lord restores and makes all things new, He wounds and heals.[26] He also brings death and makes alive.[27] Therefore, let Him destroy the yoke while reviving your spirit. It is His business to kill and destroy the works of our enemy. So stand still and watch Him move.[28]

We do not need to be found in His way. Honestly, you and I should not want to be found interfering with the Lord's business; the consequences for doing so could be grievous.[29] We can live without weights. Christ wants to use us as witnesses for Him so the weights have to go. Now is the time to let that which is dead remain dead and that which is lost remain lost. Unless the Lord chooses to resurrect the dead or reclaim the lost, settle the matter and move forward. Too much is at stake. I agree with the man of many quotes, Benjamin Franklin that after crosses and losses in our lives, we tend to grow humbler and wiser.[30] Our needed humility, wisdom and more is at stake.

Lastly, accept the newness that has come over you. Rejoice in your liberation. Move forward with Christ. You are not going forth alone. You are moving with the One in whom you are called to live, move and have your being.[31] Live and tell others of how to get through anything in Christ. You are wiser now. Get moving and teach others of the great moves of Christ our Lord.[32]

Reflection

Prayer: Holy Spirit thank you for instructing and comforting me. Show me the weight(s) to lay aside. Teach me…

_____

_____

_____

_____

_____

_____

Complete the pledge below to lay aside a weight.

_____ mourns the woman I was.

    Write Your Name

She is gone. I choose today to celebrate the woman who I am becoming in Christ Jesus. The me with weights, baggage and issues is gone. Wasted years, disappointing results and poor choices are behind me. I accept that "all" is not lost and that which remains...

_____

_____

_____

_____

_____

_____

How does the foundational scripture relate to this chapter?

{Therefore we also, since we are surrounded by so great a cloud of witnesses, let us lay aside every weight, and the sin which so easily ensnares us, and let us run with endurance the race that is set before us. Hebrews 12:1 }

_____
_____
_____
_____

Watching what you eat and exercise are pivotal to physical weight loss. Other than exercising faith in God, list at least five things that you have discovered that you must do regularly to take off spiritual weights.

1. _____
2. _____
3. _____
4. _____
5. _____
6. _____
7. _____

How can a girl or woman sabotage future victories?

_____
_____
_____
_____
_____
_____

Reread Job 5:18 and 1 Samuel 2:6. How do they impact your thinking about God?

_____

_____

_____

_____

_____

_____

_____

_____

What scripture do you plan to live off of as you plan to relinquish a particular weight? Why this one?

_____

_____

_____

_____

_____

_____

_____

_____

Share your comments and tweets on how the chapter "Taking Off The Weight" blessed you on:

https://twitter.com/StephannieBooks
http://www.blogtalkradio.com/stephanniesolomon
Facebook/Conversations With The King Ministries

Chapter Endnotes

1. Romans 3:23 For all have sinned, and come short of the glory of God. (KJV)

2. 1 John 8 and 10 If we claim to be without sin, we deceive ourselves and the truth is not in us...If we claim we have not sinned, we make him out to be a liar and his word is not in us. (NIV)

3. John 1:9 On the other hand, if we admit our sins—make a clean breast of them—he won't let us down; he'll be true to himself. He'll forgive our sins and purge us of all wrongdoing. (MSG)

4. John 20:31 But these are written that you may believe that Jesus is the Messiah, the Son of God, and that by believing you may have life in his name. (NIV)

5. Matthew 4:4 and Luke 4:4 Jesus answered by quoting Deuteronomy 8 :3: "It takes more than bread to stay alive. It takes a steady stream of words from God's mouth." (MSG)

6. Hebrews 4:12 For the Word that God speaks is alive and full of power [making it active, operative, energizing, and effective]; it is sharper than any two-edged sword, penetrating to the dividing line of the breath of life (soul) and [the immortal] spirit, and of joints and marrow [of the deepest parts of our nature], exposing and sifting and analyzing and judging the very thoughts and purposes of the heart.(AMP)

7. Psalm 119:11 I have hidden your word in my heart that I might not sin against you. (NIV)

8. James 4:17 Anyone who knows the right thing to do, but does not do it, is sinning. (NCV)

9. Psalm 34:8 Taste and see that the LORD is good; blessed is the one who takes refuge in him. (NIV)

10. Jeremiah 15:16 When your words came, I ate them; they were my joy and my heart's delight, for I bear your name, Lord God Almighty. (NIV)

11. Psalm 37:23 The steps of a good man are ordered by the LORD: and he delighteth in his way (KJV)

12. 1 Thessalonians 5:17 Pray without ceasing. (KJV)

13. Psalm 55:22 Cast your cares on the LORD and he will sustain you; he will never let the righteous be shaken. (NIV)

14. Cindy Jacobs, *Possessing the Gates of the Enemy.* Grand Rapids, Michigan. Chosen Books, 1991, 1994 and 1998.

15. Ephesians 2:10 For we are God's handiwork, created in Christ Jesus to do good works, which God prepared in advance for us to do. (NIV)

16. Galatians 5:1 Stand fast therefore in the liberty wherewith Christ hath made us free, and be not entangled again with the yoke of bondage. (KJV)

17. Luke 18:27 Jesus replied, "What is impossible with man is possible with God." (NIV)

18. Isaiah 61:3 To appoint unto them that mourn in Zion, to give unto them beauty for ashes, the oil of joy for mourning, the garment of praise for the spirit of heaviness; that they might be called trees of righteousness, the planting of the LORD, that he might be glorified. (KJV)

19. Jeremiah 32:17 "Ah, Sovereign LORD, you have made the heavens and the earth by your great power and outstretched arm. Nothing is too hard for you. (NIV)

20. Stephannie Solomon, *Living With The King: Let God Touch It*, Bloomington, Indiana, AuthorHouse, 2010, p. 37.

21. 2 Samuel 22:31a As for God, his way is perfect: (NIV)

22. Romans 8:28 That is why we can be so sure that every detail in our lives of love for God is worked into something good. (MSG)

23. Proverbs 3:5 Trust God from the bottom of your heart; don't try to figure out everything on your own. (MSG)

24. Hebrews 11:27 It was by faith that Moses left Egypt and was not afraid of the king's anger. Moses continued strong as if he could see the God that no one can see. (NCV)

25. 1 Samuel 16:1 The LORD said to Samuel, "How long will you mourn for Saul, since I

have rejected him as king over Israel? Fill your horn with oil and be on your way; I am sending you to Jesse of Bethlehem. I have chosen one of his sons to be king." (NIV)

26. Job 5:18 For he wounds, but he also binds up; he injures, but his hands also heal. (NIV)

27. 1 Samuel 2:6 The Lord kills and makes alive; He brings down to the grave and brings up (KJV)

28. 2 Chronicles 20:17 You shall not need to fight in this battle; take your positions, stand still, and see the deliverance of the Lord [Who is] with you, O Judah and Jerusalem. Fear not nor be dismayed. Tomorrow go out against them, for the Lord is with you. (AMP)

29. Acts 5:39 But if it is from God, you will not be able to stop these men; you will only find yourselves fighting against God. (NIV)

30. The Electric Ben Franklin, Independence Hall Association, http://www.ushistory.org/franklin/quotable/index.htm,ushistory.org, 1995.

31. Acts 17:28 For in him we live and move and have our being. As some of your own poets have said, We are his offspring. (NIV)

32. Daniel 12:3 The wise people will shine like the brightness of the sky. Those who teach others to live right will shine like stars forever and ever. (NCV)

Winning Women

✟

I press on toward the goal to win the [supreme and heavenly]
prize to which God in Christ Jesus is calling us upward (AMP)
Philippians 3:14

In "It" To Win "It"

Winning women see life as a race that they must win; they are in it to win it. With grace, they stand their ground, hunker down and stay the course when confronted with life's challenges. In an age of political correctness and popularity, winning women live out their convictions to be biblically correct. The Lord's grace allows winning women to go beyond speaking life. They live life in its fullness through Christ Jesus because they have learned that actions speak louder than words.[1] Even though the fullness of life may entail years of hardship, seasons of despair and memories of major faux pas, winning women rise in Jesus to accomplish HIS purpose for their lives. This is often difficult, but never impossible with the leading, wisdom and comfort of Christ's Spirit. Progress may be slow, but winning women are in it for the long haul.[2]

Keep "It" Moving

Having the operative attitude to triumph graciously in all areas of life, truly define winning women. Still, the ability to keep "it" moving during perils, affliction, hardship, and disaster is also an admirable quality of triumphant women. The "it" that is kept moving, could be the deposited dream that must come to life or the God given gift that must be boldly stirred. Like true soldiers, whatever betide, winning women continue to press forward with hope and faith in the Lord. They cosign with the Lord's servant David, that "they will not die, but live, and tell what the Lord has done," (Psalm 118:17). Like the champion Moses, they too continue strong as if they can see the God that no one can see.[3]

Keeping it moving indicates belief that the Lord will show up and show out. Winning women realize that they serve a Living God who does not lie. He promises sweet victory and He delivers. Overcoming is just on the horizon. Our later will be greater (Haggai 2:9) and the end of a matter will be better than the beginning of it (Ecclesiastes 7:8). Sisters in the faith know that come what may, if we continuously move towards our God given dream, desire and destiny; we will win. Never forget that we are of the Progressive God. In Him we live, *move* and have our being; thus, defeat really is not an option for us. We are tagged overcomers and more than conquerors. That said, get up now and get moving in Him.

Work "It"

If we look carefully at the lives of victorious women, we will find periods of ups and downs. Victory showed up because they continued to trust the Lord, using what He gave them and permitted in their lives. The gifts, grievous troubles, talents and turbulence were all used to their benefit.[4] In their memoires and transparent testimonies many women will share that they experienced bouts of anger, depression and setbacks. What sets them apart from women who settle and conform is their ability to graciously work what they have, not so much for their benefit, but for the glory of God. When the Lord Jesus is glorified and smiles on how we use what he has given to us, we and others get His benefits. We become wives, mothers, sisters, neighbors and workers with "godly benefits" that bless others.

It is the will of the Lord for each of us to work what we have been given. Christ wants us to put what He has given us to work until He comes.[5] Doing so pleases Him and affords us unique and tailored benefits. Work the dream, talent and see what the Lord does. He will blow your mind. My dear sister, do not despise nor compare your assignment or gift. Accept your individuality that has been fused with your calling and more. No one can do what you have been divinely selected to. Only you can be the blessing to those whom the Lord has placed in your circle, so work your ability to love, have mercy, listen, nurture, encourage, comfort, or make peace. There are many abilities not cited. Nonetheless, know what you possess and work it for the glory of our God. Work what you have to win.

Make "It" Happen

We are the Lord's workmanship, recreated in Him to be winners not losers.[6] He wants His disciples to win and He alone enables us to make winning happen. Because Christ gives us inner strength and grace to win, we can make anything happen, yes we can.[7] Each victory that we experience establishes us as champions, winners. Yet, each win begins with our belief that through Christ all things are possible.[8] Dreams do come true. The concept can be birthed and can thrive. Simply by "working" what the good Lord has given us makes "it" happen; we get "it" done.

Beyond believing Christ to do the impossible, is putting our faith to work. Winning women work. Their strong and enduring work ethic makes things happen in their lives. They believe that working yields great results. The foundational scripture written by the apostle Paul and given to us by the Holy Spirit connotes that winning comes from work; continual effort of pressing forward. Paul would later pen in 2 Timothy 4:7 that he fought the good fight of faith and was excited about getting his victor's crown for winning.[9] He modeled for us consistency, diligence, fortitude, faith, patience and more. Like Paul, we too can show the Lord just how much we believe Him to honor our work that is integrated with faith. Faith pleases God, but in isolation or without work it is impotent.[10]

You and I can obtain more wins than losses. When we decide that we are in our relationships, assignments and even dilemmas to triumph in Christ, we win. Victors do not quit because setbacks, diversions and hindrances come to make them immobile. Rather they use aspects of opposition to propel them to winning status. Whether they have giant gains or baby steps, winning women keep the idea or task at hand moving. With power and grace, women who win work what they have been given to the max. Working is showing the Lord just how much they believe Him to do right by them. Working the vision, gift, or assignment ultimately results in wonderful things happening for the woman of God.

Some may beg to differ with this truth, but the Lord Jesus is coming back for the winners. No one knows the day or hour scripture says, but He shall return and judge our words and deeds. Let it be known ladies that as you grew in His grace, you recognized, respected and worked what He chose to send your way. As a result the world around you witnessed your victories. They saw you winning.

Reflection

Prayer: Lord you promised me victory over sin, over death, sickness and so much more. I want to win. Sometimes I lose track that I'm on the winning team. Help me to ……..

_____
_____
_____
_____

Name at least 2 things or areas of your life that you need to work diligently? Then write the scripture(s) that you plan to declare and live by to make things happen.

_____
_____
_____
_____

Reread Mark 9:23. What does this mean to you?

_____
_____
_____
_____

Reread the Preface. What is the author's purpose? Do you see that purpose fulfilled in this chapter?

_____
_____
_____
_____
_____

How does the foundational scripture relate to this chapter?

[I press on toward the goal to win the [supreme and heavenly] prize to which God in Christ Jesus is calling us upward. Philippians 3:14]

_____

_____

_____

_____

_____

_____

_____

_____

Share your comments and tweets on how the chapter "Winning Women" blessed you on:

https://twitter.com/StephannieBooks
http://www.blogtalkradio.com/stephanniesolomon
Facebook/Conversations With The King Ministries

Chapter Endnotes

1. Stephannie Solomon, *Living With The King: Actions Speak Louder Than Words*, Bloomington, Indiana, AuthorHouse, 2010, p. 143-144.

2. Marston, Joshua, Director, *The Newsroom*, 2012.

3. Hebrews 11:27. It was by faith that Moses left Egypt and was not afraid of the king's anger. Moses continued strong as if he could see the God that no one can see. (NCV)

4. Romans 8:28. And we know that all things work together for good to them that love God, to them who are the called according to his purpose.(KJV)

5. Luke 19:12-13. There was once a man descended from a royal house who needed to make a long trip back to headquarters to get authorization for his rule and then return. But first he called ten servants together, gave them each a sum of money, and instructed them, Operate with this until I return.(MSG)

6. Ephesians 2:10. For we are God's [own] handiwork (His workmanship), recreated in Christ Jesus, [born anew] that we may do those good works which God predestined (planned beforehand) for us [taking paths which He prepared ahead of time], that we should walk in them [living the good life which He prearranged and made ready for us to live]. (AMP)

7. Philippians 4:13. I can do all things through Christ which strengtheneth me. (KJV)

8. Mark 9:23 Jesus said unto him, If thou canst believe, all things are possible to him that believeth. (KJV)

9. Philippians 4:7-8. I have fought the good (worthy, honorable, and noble) fight, I have finished the race, I have kept (firmly held) the faith.[As to what remains] henceforth there is laid up for me the [victor's] crown of righteousness [for being right with God and doing right], which the Lord, the righteous Judge, will award to me *and* recompense me on that [great] day—and not to me only, but also to all those who have loved *and* yearned for *and* welcomed His appearing (His return).(AMP)

10. James 2:20. Does some stupid person want proof that faith without deeds is useless? (CEV)

The Art Of Silence

✝

I wish you would just stop talking;
then you would really be wise! (NCV)
Job 13:5

Silence Is Golden

Emily Dickinson, an American poet, said "saying nothing sometimes says the most." Truly accomplishing this is a work in progress for most of us, especially when wronged. However, through practice of trusting the Lord for directives, we can become highly proficient at holding our peace.[1] The urge to speak our mind or get something off of our chest is not always what should be done in the moment. Sometimes we can maximize our moment by being still or being silent. Notice that I mentioned, sometimes. The proverbial saying "speech is silver and silence is golden" connotes a virtue, but not in all of life's matters. There are times when our voice should be heard, opinions known and thoughts articulated. As with all things, there should be balance with wisdom in life choices.

During my high school days a friend shared with me a saying from her teacher that I found funny at the time. Her teacher said, "silence is golden so let's be rich". At the time I knew the message that the teacher was conveying to her students, but I always felt that there was more packed within this statement. The depth of the teacher's statement would impact my life immensely in later years. Growing in God would require me to shut my mouth, even when I did not want to. I learned that to bite my tongue hurt; literally and figuratively. Taming it takes consciousness and effort because this small member of our body can cause peace and pain.[2] It is an art to subdue our tongue from speaking to soon, saying that which should never be said, or uttering hurtful words that we are unable to retract.

Decision Points

Silence is a powerful tool in many contexts and has great applications in business and other vocations. Properly used it speaks volumes. It has multiple meanings. For instance, silence could suggest compliance, guilt or consent. When the Lord instructs us to not speak on a matter, we may be viewed as cowardly, courageous, weird, but above all, wise. To save face or to keep from looking like a fool, chump, punk, wimp, push over or doormat, many women want to prove their intelligence, age and strength by vocalizing their opinion. What many sisters fail to realize is that wisdom is proven to be right by what it does.[3] Silence is the genius of fools and one of the virtues of the wise.[4] More often than not, it is wise and better to outwit others and preserve our peace and dignity by simply keeping our mouths shut. Herein, we actually increase the power of our voice as we use our silence to be heard.

As we live to become women after God's heart, we must admit that it is not easy to keep our mouths shut when confronted with personal and social injustices. It is also difficult to remain silent when angry, afraid and/or falsely accused. Remaining silent during such times is not always appropriate, but when it is befitting, mum's the word. We can do this. We can do all things through Christ which strengthens us and it strengthens us to be silent sometimes. Growing to the point of knowing when to zip it, seal our lips, and shut our trap can prove helpful on so many fronts.

It is unfortunate that many girls and women do not have holy female role models who gracefully exhibit before them silence under pressure. If anything, there is massive exposure of loudmouthed women in the home, school, church, workplace, and on reality and tabloid talk shows who bully and fight their way through ordeals. However, I like what I heard actor Denzel Washington say in the movie "American Gangster" as he portrayed Frank Lucas. He said, "The loudest one in the room is usually the weakest one in the room".[5] This statement speaks volumes. One of the ways that it speaks to us is that being vociferous without godly directives shows contenders that we lack such things as confidence, discipline, intelligence, and a healthy self-image. While our flesh and foes will try to provoke us to speak untimely and out of character, it is profitable for us to hold our peace. Thus, it is important ladies to know our triggers and hot spots. The enemy knows them and will use our unresolved matters, sore spots to rub us the wrong way. In these divine moments the Lord will speak for us, whether through others or life events. He will get the glory and we will win.

Holding our peace is arduous sometimes, but it can become an art in our lives. Know that there is only one who has modeled this principle masterfully and He is The Master, Jesus Christ. He has left for us His witness, showing us how to do this and why we must implement this discipline in our lives. Jesus did not verbally respond to every accusation and question. He evidences the art of silence in His life when a host of accusers and conspirators brought Him before Pilate. The scriptures reveal, "So again Pilate asked him, Aren't you going to answer? See how many things they are accusing you of. But Jesus still made no reply, and Pilate was amazed." (Mark 15:4-5) Earlier in time the Holy Spirit revealed in Isaiah 53:7, "He was oppressed and afflicted, yet He did not open His mouth; He was led like a lamb to the slaughter, and as a sheep before her shearers is silent, so He did not open his mouth."

Sisters we are called and chosen to be imitators of Christ.[6]

There is strength in discerning when to be silent. As women of Christ, we must know when to speak and when to refrain from speaking. There is wisdom in knowing the difference and living out the godly choice. Contention, discord and so much more could be avoided just for a moment of silence.

Be Still

The art of silence extends beyond not speaking. Simply being physically still works to bring drama down and calm our nerves. Oftentimes this requires great intention on our part because there are so many contenders of peace. Turn off and unplug the electronic devices and close the windows and the doors. Be strategic when planning to be still and quiet. Know that you are coming before God. If you are expecting family or guests soon, this may not be the best time to get quiet. Have a plan. Keep in mind that you do not have to spend hours in stillness unless the Spirit of the Lord is leading you this way. You will be amazed at what 5 minutes of alone time with the Lord will accomplish. I believe that our speaking should be minimal, quoting only affirmations from the Lord at the beginning or end of the quiet time.

Know that everything that sounds good and empowering is not an affirmation for Christians. Godly affirmations must be true. Where else is truth, but in the Word of God. For some this is considered meditation.[7] You don't need to chant, hum and have candles to meditate. You do need the word of God, for the prince of the power of the air will attempt to whisper deceptions in your ear. Cover yourself; therefore, in silence with the words of our Christ, His blood and His name.

Now that you have held your peace and set still before God, stand still and witness His salvation.[8] In your stillness know that He alone is God.[9] Allow Him to lead, speak and fend for you.[10] If He chooses to give you the words to say, accept and speak them.[11] He is justice as much as He is love, peace wisdom and truth. Lastly, confess your fault or sin to God if you have spoken out of turn. Embrace His forgiveness and grace. Don't spend another minute replaying how you spoke in haste, hostility and hurt. It was done and you felt terrible about it. Repent and ask the Lord to show you how to move forward from your moment of loose lips. He will. Continual practice of stillness and quietness in Christ will eventually prove that one has mastered the art of silence.

Reflection

Prayer: Lord there is so much to learn about you and from you. In silence I should here you, but the issues of life are constantly speaking to me. Show me how to be still and…….

_____
_____
_____
_____
_____
_____
_____
_____

What are the benefits of holding your peace?

_____
_____
_____

Reread Luke 7:35. How can this scripture be a challenge to a Woman of God?

_____
_____
_____
_____

How does the foundational scripture relate to this chapter?

{I wish you would just stop talking;
then you would really be wise! Job 13:5}

_____

_____

_____

_____

Reread the Preface. Is this chapter disciple-centric? How so?

_____

_____

_____

_____

**Share your comments and tweets on how the chapter
"The Art Of Silence" blessed you on:**

https://twitter.com/StephannieBooks
http://www.blogtalkradio.com/stephanniesolomon
Facebook/Conversations With The King Ministries

Chapter Endnotes

1. Luke 12:11-12 When you are brought before synagogues, rulers and authorities, do not worry about how you will defend yourselves or what you will say, for the Holy Spirit will teach you at that time what you should say.(NIV)

2. James 3:5-10 It only takes a spark, remember, to set off a forest fire. A careless or wrongly placed word out of your mouth can do that. By our speech we can ruin the world, turn harmony to chaos, throw mud on a reputation, send the whole world up in smoke and go up in smoke with it, smoke right from the pit of hell. This is scary: You can tame a tiger, but you can't tame a tongue—it's never been done. The tongue runs wild, a wanton ºkiller. With our tongues we bless God our Father; with the same tongues we curse the very men and women he made in his image. Curses and blessings out of the same mouth! (MSG)

3. Luke 7:35 But wisdom is proved to be right by what it does. (NCV)

4. Bernard De Bonnard; *Hoyt's New Cyclopedia of Practical Quotations.* New York, London: Funk & Wagnalls Company, 1922; Bartleby.com, 2009.

5. American Gangster. Prod. Brian Grazer. Perf. Denzel Washington. Universal Studios, 2007.

6. Ephesians 5:1 Watch what God does, and

then you do it, like children who learn proper behavior from their parents. (MSG)

7. Joshua 1:8 This Book of the Law shall not depart out of your mouth, but you shall meditate on it day and night, that you may observe and do according to all that is written in it. For then you shall make your way prosperous, and then you shall deal wisely and have good success. (AMP)

8. 2 Chronicles 20:17 You shall not need to fight in this battle; take your positions, stand still, and see the deliverance of the Lord [Who is] with you, O Judah and Jerusalem. Fear not nor be dismayed. Tomorrow go out against them, for the Lord is with you. (AMP)

9. Psalm 46:10 Be still, and know that I am God: I will be exalted among the heathen, I will be exalted in the earth. (KJV)

10. Exodus 14:14 The LORD will fight for you; you need only to be still." (NIV)

11. Matthew 10:19 But when they deliver you up, do not worry about how or what you should speak. For it will be given to you in that hour what you should speak. (AMP)

Let's Talk About Sex

✝

There's an opportune time to do things, a right time for everything on the earth...A right time to shut up and another to speak up. (MSG)

It's Not A Dirty Word

There's an opportune time to do things, a right time for everything on the earth. Jesus refers to the importance of timing when He said, "My time has not yet come".[1] Even the end times is synchronized.[2] As mentioned in the previous chapter, there is a right time to be silent. However, there is also a time to be vocal; timing is everything. That said, let's talk about sex. Many Women of God are not meeting success in the area of sex. Many are unfulfilled and passing on sexual dysfunctions to their sons and daughters. Confusion and perversion are walking hand in hand as particular tolerances and acceptances work to redefine God's standards about sex. Many unmarried women are flaunting their sexual exploits and many married women are living sexually frustrated lives. Sadder still, Christian women, who are supposed to live victoriously, make up a significant portion of these two groups.

Ladies no one can explain your perception of sex or your sexual experiences like you. Certainly a man cannot. When sisters are truly comfortable with one another, talking about certain matters becomes easy. Sometimes females share too much information (TMI) with the wrong sister because there is the desire to get out that which has been a form of torment for years. The stories are vast that lie within each woman and girl as they relate to sex. Oh, if vaginas could talk, what would their stories consist of? Would they speak of abuses beyond human comprehension? What would they share about individual proclivities and pasts? Would they speak of longing for fulfillment as the Lord intended? Just what would they say or scream.

Let us understand that the word sex and the act of sex are not meant to be evil. Sex is a creation of God our Father, not humans. It was meant to feel good and be enjoyed within the perimeter of holy marriage. Mothers and female mentors cannot control the sexual decisions of daughters and female mentees, but there is the window of influence that can be used to create talking points with them. If the Mothers of the Church would really testify and mentor the younger women properly, their testimonies would truly bless. I believe that many unplanned pregnancies would not occur and girls would not repeat the sins of their mothers and mothers' parents if Christian women who lived through the disadvantages of sex outside of marriage would speak up and out more often about this behavior. I am very aware that this is a sensitive and quiet subject and that many Christian women feel unqualified to speak out against fornication and sexual immorality because of their secrets and fears, but the apostle Paul is a great example of how the Lord can and will use anyone to get the job done with holy boldness. See Acts 22.

God's Women have to be delivered and made whole to render sound and sanctified advice. They cannot be bleeding from guilt and shame from their past's sins and give strong sound council. Neither should they live arrogantly with their sin, believing that so many women do or have done the same sin which makes them exempt from self-examination, healthy shame, confession and repentance. It is the lack of these afore mentioned acts that has created repeat offenders and communities of women raising children alone, some being by different men. Loving on the children once they are here is good. It is what the mother is supposed to do. The child did not ask to be born and did not choose the parents. So no mother is doing a child a favor by taking good care of them. This is her reasonable service. Yet, at some point accountability, responsibility, discipline and sanctification has to kick in. Sex before marriage with a man or woman certainly is not the Lord's way for women, but it happens. There is no upside to having sex before marriage. If we think of one, will it line up with the will and Word of God? One downside is that you lose the wonder and thrill of sharing something precious with your God appointed husband.

In no way am I advocating condemnation against women who have children out of wedlock. I am a product of such behavior and grew up seeing it manifested in my community. Neither am I promoting abortion, hysterectomies, genital mutilation and other ways to prevent pregnancy. God's grace is present for the poor decisions and sins that each of us commit. Let me be clear also in sharing that I am not endorsing stunted growth, where a woman lives and waddles in her sin because of shame and guilt. Mistakes happen because everything is not so cut and dry; black or white. Yet there is a difference when we witness once an incident, twice a coincidence and three times a pattern. It is the pattern that becomes generational and socially acceptable. Everything lawful or socially accepted is not in alignment with the ways of our God. (See 1 Corinthians 6:12 and 1 Corinthians 10:23). In all honesty many Christian women who have had children out of wedlock are not delivered from the sting of their sins. They do a lot of overcompensating and deflecting in order to dismiss the sin. Because they are not healed and delivered by Christ, the godly conversations are not being spoken to the needed ears of boys, girls, women and men. Thus, the sins of sexual immorality continue without embarrassment, conviction and correction.

Just as sex is not a dirty word, neither are the words virgin and abstinence. Society has concluded that these words are dirty as perversions and immorality are flaunted as admirable traits. Many communities and cultures are not instilling in children, youth and adults the value of abstaining from sex outside of marriage and living proudly as a virgin. Teachings on the high premium of virginity and abstinence is minimized and often silenced. Promotion and glorification of sexual promiscuity and experimentation is the norm. Even whoredom is glorified through various mediums such as pornographic acting, video vixens, and mistresses known also as "the other woman". That which is perverse and outside of the will of God is often lauded, while that which is pure and within the will of God is slated as dull and undesirable. Molestation, rape and seductions steadily increase especially on the young and innocent because sexual perversions are pervasive.

Destruction or spoiling innocence in young girls has always been the design of Satan. When innocence is lost through rape and molestation, it is assumed that girls are less likely to discover what sex should be like in the Lord. Statistics reveal that many girl rape victims become sexually promiscuous teenagers or women. They tend to view their vaginas as a means to some type of gain. Also, girls who believe the lies of Satan and the world that it is fine to hasten the blossoming process by giving themselves to every charmer, are likely to become bitter, depressed, confused and resentful women. We are created to bloom, but not too soon.[3] There is a time for every stage of life. Awakening sexual feelings in an immature soul is devious and dangerous. Trying to hurry love through sex stirs emotions and causes arousals that are complex to adults and even more to children. There is a level of responsibility and maturity that should accommodate sexual activity. Whether we want to admit it or not, the emotional self is often tied to the sexual self. When immature and irresponsible females become sexually active, they set themselves up to be emotionally wounded and undone. Only in Christ is such damage repaired, yet so much emotional pain can be avoided by waiting and not hurrying what looks like love.

A warped perception of love and sex is one of Satan's desires for girls and women. Sadly, for many women a distorted view of sex has led to a perverted and promiscuous lifestyle. Molestation, promiscuity, perversion and rape have stolen their innocence and awakened, way too early, sexual feelings that are meant to be experienced in the confines of holy matrimony. Here innocence is not synonymous to ignorance. It means guiltless and pure. For varied reasons innocence of millions of boys and girls is lost early in life. Case in point, sexual orientation is declared by elementary aged and middle school aged children. In other words, they have declared to prefer having sexual relations with someone of either the same or opposite sex. To prefer anything means that you have sampled both and select one over the other. Thus, children, teens and women are participating in sexual activities in order to make such a determination or declaration.

Christ gives grace to be a virgin. Through His grace He is able to keep us from falling.[4] He strengthens girls and women to abstain from sexual relations outside of His will. He is able to help those who are being tempted and pressured.[5] Many girls say that peer pressure makes it impossible to refrain from having sex before the appointed time and grown women wrestle with the same. As true as the struggle is to refrain, the power of Christ is able to keep any of us in such struggles while giving us peace and joy.[6] Lest we forget, there are women who have been sexually active and know what pleasures they are called to denounce. Difficult as it may be, Children of God can do all things through Christ which strengthens us and it strengthens us to be free of sexual immorality.

For the millions of women and girls whose sexual innocence has been stolen, know that the love of God is still available to you. Nothing can separate us from His love.[7] Virginity in the physical sense will not be regained, but the grace of God works to restore your dignity and self-worth. Grace is powerful in reestablishing the Lord's people. It makes us new and what has happened becomes our past that God miraculously uses to His glory and for our betterment. We all can find grace in the eyes of the Lord. Our sinful acts and gross offenses may work to make us feel dirty and worthless, but the Lord is available and ready to destroy the shame, guilt and recklessness that threaten to mar our perception of Christ. We were created with value and worth in mind. Rape, molestation and seduction intend to rob females of these virtues, but God's grace is so much greater. The world's view of virgin and abstinence is a reflection of how hostile it is to the pure ways of God. Giving ourselves away to the things of this world that devalue females has tremendous consequences. However, holding out, waiting to give one's self sexually to another who has been ordained by the Lord yields unique rewards.

The Safety Net

No one can make us feel safe or come to our rescue like Christ Jesus. It is in the safety of His arms that we are comforted and kept. Surely many parents, friends and loved ones have great intentions, efforts and love, but they can never do what God does through Christ Jesus and His Holy Spirit. Never! Statistics and social science show that when children do not feel safe their young and impressionable minds take matters into their own hands. Families, communities and society as a whole witness an evolution of sorrow, fear, withdrawal, hostility, depression, violence, self-sabotage, self-destruction, and other behaviors that we label as acting out. Children are born trusting; their dependence on their caregiver is not optional. When trust is broken through varied abuses and neglect, negative psychological ramifications are sure to follow.

Knowing that we are built this way, the enemies of God work early in our lives to destroy trust. This process continues throughout life because destruction is never content with one act of infidelity and distrust.[8] Anti-Christ spirits thrive in disbelief, distrust, desolation, depravity, decadence and the like. Their goal is to consume human thoughts and our hearts with things meant to work against the love of God, loyalty to God as well as the life and legacy of His Son, Jesus Christ. If they are successful with their mission, the gospel of Christ will be rejected; spiritual blinders will remain on human eyes and many will live a reprobate life. The same holds true in a marriage or business partnership. Infidelity is always meant to heighten feelings of disconnect and insecurity. Safety becomes an issue whenever trust has been broken.

There are countless spoken and secret accounts of violated trusts among women. Sexual violations in particular have occurred when girls and women were clueless to the deceptive intentions of their male and/or female abusers. Thus, parents, guardians, caregivers and husbands are to make daughters, sisters and wives feel safe, not threatened. Forcing or manipulating a female to engage in any sex act is not the assurance of safety. Any girl or woman who believes that true safety comes from someone who requires sex of them, within or without the confines of marriage, using coercion or seduction is misled. Christ does not force, intimidate, manipulate or use deception of any kind to woo and win us to Himself. Having a relationship with Him never involves seduction. He is honest and open with us from beginning to end. God, who is our refuge, needs no tricks to win our confidence. Sisters know that the God in the person who is interacting with us should make us feel genuinely safe, especially if the person is our father, fiancé, brother, husband, uncle, god-father or son.

Incidentally, fathers, fiancés, brothers, husbands, uncles, god-fathers and sons should cover their daughters, fiancées, sisters, wives, nieces, god-daughters and mothers. They should always have their back and these women ought to know it.[9] Doing so is not something extra. It is; however, an expectation of his reasonable service.[10] This is what he is supposed to do. It is doing the right thing. Family members, former girlfriends, flirtatious fans, friends and foes should not be allowed to speak against them, particularly the wife. She is the one who the husband has left his parents for. He has chosen to unite with her permanently.[11] A wife is a reflection of her husband; she is his choice. Leaving her open to attacks is a sad commentary of his maturity and love for God. Husbands who take good care of their wives and wives who take good care of their husbands display true worship to God. Moreover, ladies look for signs of authentic acts of protection during the dating process, especially when in the company of your date's family, friends and acquaintances. Ask questions until you feel safe.[12] Dating and questions go together. Do not assume what he thinks or where the relationship is going. Assumptions will make you look foolish. As stated by one of my favorite preachers, "Assumptions are termites of a relationship".[13] In addition, do not be deceived by detours in the conversations that are deflections from being truthful to you.

It is ok to want to be and feel safe in a relationship. Something is gravely wrong if instability and danger makes one feel comfortable. In the world of dating, know that safety features or lack of them are indicators of a possible mate, mismatched marriage or a rocky start. This is applicable to the young woman who dates as well as the older woman who may be dating after years of being married and now you are widowed or divorced. Times are not what they once were. HIV and STD's are real and rampant. Next to African American gay and bisexual men, women in developing countries over the age of 40 are leading the pack in HIV infections.[14] The epidemic has increased most dramatically among women of color, especially black women. In 2005, women of color accounted for 80% of all women estimated to be living with AIDS; black women made up 62% of this total.[15]

For readers who have sons, love them enough to teach them the importance of making their significant other or wife safe, not insecure. Although they are not responsible for how a woman receives what he does, he is responsible in assuring her that with him she is safe. Let him know that when a woman says ***NO! STOP!*** that it does not mean ***No, Don't Stop!*** Share with him that even if she does not do the right thing, he can and should do the right thing, for security and respect are cut from the same cloth. A woman needs to know that she can trust a man.

Subsequently, if trust is broken in any relationship, incrementally or instantly, it can be restored by the power of the Living God. When the Lord desires the continuance of any relationship, He will rebuild the bond as needed. He is the Master Builder. For many individuals this is a large and hard pill to swallow, for regaining trust is difficult. Yet, Christians must remember that there is nothing impossible with God.[16] Relations that are meant to be should be healthy. They are meaningful, support the God in us and are non-partakers of our flesh driven goals. Still, trusting others is problematic for many because tolerance in society has swayed many to believe that we must involve certain individuals in our lives regardless of their dysfunctions. Being a public servant in two school systems, I have witnessed various abuses towards children from uncaring parents and caregivers. Biological connectivity does not always and automatically denote care, love, support, compassion, encouragement and security. Most bonds of trust are broken from family members. However, the Lord Jesus is available and willing to show His women servants how to press and move forward without the baggage of family dysfunction. We are given grace to endure varied abuses, but we are called to rise above abuse as well as our abusers.

Ladies some relationships were not meant to be. Every desire should not be pursued. Let the Spirit of the Lord Jesus guide and correct your decisions. He can do it. He regulates, restores, removes and replaces with pure excellence. Trust His choice. If Christ decides that the relationship remains, trust Him to strengthen you to not allow roots of dysfunctions to overtake and overwhelm you. No generational curse is the boss of you, Christ is. Trust Him to shut it down. Habitual choices will not win as Christ is permitted total sovereignty of your heart. We can trust again, yes we can. Even if we follow the Russian proverb and signature phrase adopted and made famous by former President Ronald Reagan, *trust but verify*, we can move forward in divinely placed relationships. Without being overly suspect, which can hinder moving forward, you and I should verify that behaviors are sincere, information shared is accurate or that a person is trustworthy. It is ok to ask the Lord to prove authenticity from even the most popular and reliable person. It is possible that patterns and history will reveal undesirable habits again. Some say that once is an incident twice is a coincidence three times a pattern or you fool me once shame on you fool me twice shame on me. Check out the source ladies.

Know that being preventive and proactive does a sister well. Telling girls that they are precious is a start. Early in life they need to be taught that they are not just gifted, but that they are gifts to their families, communities and to our world. Reassurances will be necessary as they make mistakes and encounter opposing views along the way. In addition, it is essential that they are educated in the ways of respect; respect for themselves, others and the things of God. Only then will they recognize when they are being respected or disrespected. Moreover, families, mentors, and guardians need to instill in young boys who may become a husband and/or father that real men cover their wives and daughters. There are multiple ways to show safety other than physical protection. Males should be taught to financially protect their wives and dependent children in case of their absence. Having working health and life insurance policies are one of several ways to protect them. Making his mother, sister, female date, wife and daughter feel safe is just the right thing to do. This aspect of chivalry is not dead. Creating a feeling of security, a safety net for a female truly is a fine quality in any male date or mate.

I'z Married Now

Some say that every date is a potential mate. This saying may not have much weight in certain parts of the world because so many women desire fame, fortune, job security and children prior to entering marriage. Sadly, this saying has little to no meaning to the child brides in Ethiopia, Afghanistan, India, Yemen, Saudi Arabia and other countries who are being married off to old men; men who these children would have more than likely never chose as their groom. Child marriage and child betrothal customs are instances where force rather than personal choice has brought the bride and groom together.[17] In spite of this type of coming together, the mention of a wedding is still cause for celebration nearly everywhere. Even those who profess an alternative lifestyle and exchange the truth about God for a lie desire a festive and celebratory wedding ceremony. Despite the variety of views on marriage, celebrating the joining of two lives during the wedding ceremony remains a big deal in the world.

For many Christian women getting married is a cure-all to several problems. Four of those problems are being forsaken, fornication, famine and financial crisis. Having signed the license and exchanged rings, many sisters proudly profess like the character Shug in the novel *The Color Purple*, "I'z married now".[18] They can have sex now as often as desired, without conviction and inhibition. A host of single ladies who are saved and the married who are sexually starved, view marriage as a time to have sex and lots of it. For the men and women reading this, please stop believing the misinformation regarding women and sex. Don't get the facts twisted. Women who enjoy having sex are not sluts, whores and nymphomaniacs. Women who fall in these categories tend to enjoy other things more than sexual activity. For many of them having sex is just a vehicle to attaining something else. Our mothers, grandmothers, Mothers of the Church, female preachers, pastors, sisters, and wives may not like who they are having sex with, but they desire it and like men, think of it often.

In other words, the women who we assume are unassuming, desire great sex and lots of it. They like starting and ending their day with it. Yes, child rearing and work can tire mothers out, but work tires a man out also. Women do not just want Calgon to take them away. Pornography is not just a husband's problem. Cyber affairs are just as real and common for women as they are for men. Women have always stepped out on men. However, the standards and mores set by men have been established to protect their egos. Even now stoning women, setting them on fire for adultery is permitted in certain parts of the world. As much as attitudes have changed in some "civilized" nations, there still exist double standards when it comes to women having multiple sex partners and seeking sexual fulfillment within and outside of marriage. In 2012 sexual assertiveness by Christian women, church going women is very much alive. Yet, many of these women are frustrated because their assertions are often misunderstood and threatening. God's chosen vessels are trying to find fun and fulfillment in holiness with words like kinky, freak, erotic, and bondage circulating in their heads and their place of sexual activities.

With all of this being said, sex is just as important, if not more, to women as it is to men. Yes we tend to be more emotional and romantic, but women want to talk about sex and be in the business of having great sex with their husbands. Great sex does a marriage good. Yet, a healthy marriage is not built on great and frequent sex alone. One of several truths about holy marriage is that husbands and wives must learn to think relationally. Getting to the point of experiencing fulfillment in the sexual arena comes from intentionally focusing on strengthening the marital relationship.

Commitment, security, devotion, patience, forgiveness, fidelity, communication, and humor are some components that make "having sex" grow to "fulfilling sex." It is all about relationship building. This means that the husband and wife avail themselves to the new and complex personality of the other person, their spouse. They are literally making room for each other, assets and dysfunctions included. Learning to share every aspect of one's world is the charted course. This can be a daunting task when self-discovery and personal evolution in Christ is ongoing. However, each spouse must choose to invest in the marriage and believe in each other as they learn and change. A reminder of each spouse's purpose in the other's life is seen through openly displayed pictures of each other, the wearing of wedding rings, daily chats and more. Life for both spouses has purposeful inclusiveness. No one should be surprised to know that either spouse is married. It has amazed me to learn that certain individuals were married only after hearing that their spouse died. They were not seen out and about as a couple and conversations did not expose that there was a marriage. There should not be a life with the spouse and life without the spouse or friends and funds that are not intended to meet the spouse. Exclusiveness and selfishness must give way to inclusiveness and selflessness when getting married. There is no holding out and as the scriptures state neither should hold back nor defraud the another.[19]

I firmly believe that many Christians enter marriage not understanding that giving of oneself to the spouse and serving the spouse are acts of selflessness and worship to God. Expecting one's sexual and emotional needs to be met by one's spouse is desiring godly service from one's mate. Many Christian couples do not have godly role models, have not been taught that marriage is larger than a contract and that giving of oneself emotionally, intellectually, spiritually and sexually are acts of worship to God. This is the building of a healthy relationship. It is ongoing and for many it is work that they are not committed to. Yet this way of marital living is our reasonable service; the spiritual way for us to worship God.[20] This is what we are supposed to do as married people.

How we perceive sex in marriage and God in sex strongly influence marital success and marital retardation. As new creatures in Christ how we saw sex before following His lead becomes very different and new.[21] Notice that I said becomes. Our understanding in this area evolves as we grow in Christ. This means that whatever the world has exposed to us never matches the blueprint of God Our Architect. If anything, the world takes what the Lord has ordained and creates an alternative; it exchanges the truth about God for a lie. God has ordained sex to be enjoyed by a male husband and female wife. Scripturally referencing the husband as a human male (having 46 chromosomes, the sex chromosomes paired as X and Y) and the wife as a human female (having also 46 chromosomes with the sex chromosomes paired as X and X). Dressing up the exterior, changing names and surgically reconstructing the original genitalia does not change the inner highly organized structure that has been created by our All Wise and All Knowing God.

God is about building strong relationships, holy covenants. Marriage is intended to be holy because God is holy.[22] As with all things that the Lord has ordained, the enemies of Christ have strategically worked to pervert them. Sex outside of marriage is forbidden by the Lord for various reasons. God's rationale intends to protect us physically, psychologically, spiritually, and emotionally. Having sex with a man or woman links us to them. Sexual encounters outside of holy matrimony links us in sin as well as with another person's baggage. Also each sexual experience leaves impressions on our thoughts and emotions that defy being expunged. Every memory of sexual encounters becomes a comparison to the other. The Lord God intended for sex to join us; however, we were not intended to be joined with everyone sexually, having a little bit of everyone traveling with us.

Sex before the vow to wed can shake and shatter the core of intimacy between a husband and wife in which only Christ can restore. Sleeping with an intended mate can potentially dissolve a marriage before it gets off of the ground because the development of marital intimacy has been arrested by previous unordained sexual encounters. As an associate of mine stated, "If you keep insisting on putting the cart before the horse eventually somebody is gonna get run over!"[23] Every look, touch and word has the potential to trigger a flashback of people and experiences that have no business in any marriage. Three or more truly is a crowd. Ghosts from the past rise up to torment and even direct in what a wife should allow and do in the relationship with her husband. Having witnessed what Satan strives to achieve, let us consider the perfect way of the Lord.

Christ wants couples to grow in Him and to grow together. He is very much aware that the attack on intimacy leads to disconnect, infidelity, pornography and other agents of marital discord and destruction. So He extends His grace to all of us, that we will receive it, stand in it and grow in it. We need grace to move beyond the errors of our pasts and grace to succeed in marriage. As it pertains to sexual attitudes and fulfillment in marriage, grace is there too. God and His grace do not disappear because wives are having sex with their husbands. He said that He would never leave or forsake us.[24] He is there, but He wants to be welcomed. His presence is not going to take fun and enjoyment out of the sex act. He wants to be acknowledged in every way.[25] Acknowledging Him includes the bedroom just as much as in the boardroom and church house. He desires to make the husband and wife one.[26] A problem with many Christian wives is that they are not inviting Christ into the bedroom. The ghosts of the pasts and images from the world are entertained and even acted out. The possibilities of sexual fulfillment in Jesus somehow seem inappropriate; hence, many saints just don't connect the two, God and sex.

Holy marriage is not all about sex, but sex within marriage was designed by the Lord. This is not man's law. Remember, the Lord is a relationship builder. Sexual intimacy works to build a marriage. It is a form of communication and connectedness. Ladies, if you ever want to make a point of just how ticked off you are with your husband, stop having sex with him. This is not a good choice by far, but women, and men by the way, have used this selfish tactic for years. Although unspoken, the spouse who is defrauding and holding back on the other sexually is sending messages. Again, it is not a good and godly choice at all because the negative ramifications will be shared by both spouses. Turning your back to your spouse in bed, while angry, does not do a marriage good. Trust God sisters and turn the matter that troubles you over to Him.

The excitement about getting married has to transfer into and continue in the marriage. How the husband and wife decide to maintain that thrill is up to the two of them. Each spouse is evolving and so is the marriage. There should be enthusiasm about a shared future. When the flame dims and the thrill is gone, do not give in or give up. This is not the time, nor the place to throw in the towel.[27] Rather continue to pray and seek wisdom and guidance from the One who created and ordained the marriage. Furthermore, use caution when seeking advice from others, regardless of who they are. Everyone cannot identify with your journey. Troubles will surface, but continue to always make the One responsible for the union your confidant. A threefold cord is not easily broken.[28] This does not mean that the Lord will not use people to pour wisdom, encouragement and more into you. He does all things well.

To so many people marriage is just a contract with benefits until they are ready to break it. Christ was never in it for them. In Christ, marriage is a covenant. Contract and covenant are not the same. Unlike the contract, the covenant is not easily broken because it is three fold rather than two against the world. Having Christ fighting with and for you in the marriage is more than a spouse fighting alone or two people fighting without the blessing of Jesus Christ --- Ecclesiastes 4:12.

Learn to be discerning of what is read, viewed and heard. Know what to tune out and respectfully dismiss when others take the liberty to speak death over your marriage. There are people who like to speak on things that they are clueless about. Open your spirit to the ways of Christ all the more during the craziest of times and marital discord. Believe only the ways of the Lord even when they are unpopular, peculiar and seemingly contradictory. To do these things is living life as a game changer. You and I are not expected to respond as people who do not know and love the Lord.

Our responses in Him will raise eyebrows, turn heads and provoke questions about us and our behavior. Be willing to let Christ use you to show the difference between faith and a farce. The journey may not be simple, but there is a reward and a shout of triumph awaiting anyone who puts their trust in the Lord. Kim Kardashian's marriage to Kris Humphries was a farce. However, any marriage that is built on all of the Word of God exemplifies faith. As strange as God's ways are, they are perfect.[29] There are ways that seem right to us and others, but if the plan has not come from the Lord, it will fail.[30] There are many who wish for the dissolution of marriage, especially Christian unions because misery does love company.

I have witnessed so many Christian couples seek assistance from sincere and loving Christians only to be misinformed and misguided. There are divorced persons who have not learned from their marital errors or have not been healed of their hurt, giving unsound marital advice. Among us are women who are married to either unsaved or carnal Christian men offering wives tales and slogans instead of the Word of God for counsel. Also in the group of advisors are a select group of Church leaders who give worldly options to wives that include "do you" over "do Jesus". Then there are the single ladies who speak on and against marriages with disdain and ignorance. Sisters love each other, but know that married women and single women have two different lifestyles and callings. If you have to share with a Sister Girl or Girl Friend, be discerning, prayerful, and selective.

I dare to share that there is so much wrong information being shared within the Body of Christ in regard to marriage. As I stated earlier, many people are putting the cart before the horse; they are working backwards and expect the

Lord to bless their mess and disobedience. Because various governments have made it lawful to marry someone of the same gender and chromosomes, many who profess to live by every word of the Lord are in agreement with human law rather than God's way. They have exchanged the truth about God for a lie. The influential slang "It's Your Thing, Do What You Wanna Do" created by the American musical group the Isley Brothers has permeated every aspect of life not just in the American culture, but throughout. It includes the Body of Christ. The severe breakdown and alteration of marriage is endorsed by pockets of spiritual advisors who have been and remain unsuccessful in marriage. Their marriages are dysfunctional and they intentionally live in defiance to the Spirit of God in this area. How can someone who engineers unbiblical reasons to dishonor the Lord in marriage wholly council those whose marriages are sick?

In addition to what has been shared, celebrations and publicity for the long marriages are minimal and low key. They deserve shout outs, awards and front page exposure. There is little to no godly information being shared by those who have attained victories in their marriage. This is such a sad commentary on the Bride of Jesus Christ. The order of God is for the wise and older Women of Faith to teach the younger women.[31] We are to comfort as we have been comforted.[32] It is this divine blueprint that is a prescription for success in marriage as well as other areas of our lives. To negate what the Lord has put in place is foolish and a reflection of bondage. Why allow someone to lead us who lacks wisdom and foresight? This is merely allowing the blind to lead others who are in the same condition.[33] My sister it is not the Lord's will that any of us be ignorant and led astray. The report of the Lord out shines and outweighs anything that is said by anyone. His report to us and the world is of hope, love, faith, restoration, reconciliation, redemption, forgiveness, integrity, obedience, commitment, fidelity, passion, relationship, followship, discipline, kindness, triumph, mercy and grace. If any advice is sought out, we ought to seek the thoughts and ways of Christ. We should hear at least one of these attributes of Christ in the conversation.

God knew exactly what He had in mind when He made woman. We are constructed to be emotional beings; receivers. Does this mean that we have excuses to sound off on others every chance that we get? Absolutely not. Neither does being a receiver connote that we are doormats and are here to take abuses from anyone at will. Some of us are a little more touchy feely than others, but connecting emotionally with others is what we do. If this part of our being is not corrupted, we do this well. Yet, for many of us emotions tend to drive us. We think with our heart, and follow our heart. Being emotional and sensitive has its fine points and place, but we are to follow Christ not our heart.[34] Hollywood produces movies and Harlequin publishes books that strongly emphasize the need for individuals to follow their heart. This is the way of the world. The way of the Lord is, He looks in the heart of every one and desires that we follow Him. Society will, say that we should always and can follow our emotions, heart or feelings. Yes we can, but we should not. If women and girls had sex with everyone they had emotional and/or sexual "feelings" for, how would this honor the Lord? Moreover, where is the Lord glorified in our decision to follow our emotional self? [35] Our emotional self has importance, but should never lead us, for if we are not careful and discerning, we will become emotionally intimate with people who do not empower us. What we need from them will corrupt us and we may even find our saved selves participating in acts that are relegated to a post at the fringes of darkness. Connected to the wrong people, emotional intimacy can be worse than sexual intimacy outside of marriage.

Just as feelings do not drive and define faith; they do not drive or define a healthy marriage. Feelings flutter, fade, fail and are fickle. Happiness is a feeling, but it is contingent on a happening. As much as some pretend to be happy, no one is happy all of the time. So joy that is unspeakable has to kick in when the happenings of life do not warrant a happy face. Joy helps the mature woman ride the waves of life. It is permanence whereas happiness is temporal. In no way am I implying that happiness should be minimized. Every sound minded spouse wants a happy marriage. However, the storms of life have a way of rocking marriages. Being happy will not secure a sound mind during the turbulent times; the joy of the Lord will. It will strengthen the marriage and the two called to it. [36] Joy will outlast the sensations of sex and contribute to triumphant living. How great will be our joy in the victories that the Lord shall give us.[37]

In one's excitement to be married be prepared to be a prayer warrior. Marriage is not for wimps. Anything and anyone can be used to cause division and dissolve. If the union is Christ ordained, the weapons formed against it may be vast, but know that what the Lord has joined together let no one separate.[38] As a conqueror you have the authority to prevent spirits of separatism to prosper in your marriage. Fight in the spirit with much prayer. It would be excellent if spouses prayed together. If not the case, know that one can chase a thousand. Great things happen when a person living right prays, especially in marriages.

Reflection

Prayer: Father show me how to view sex. I want to enjoy everything that you have ordained. I tend to....

_____
_____
_____
_____

Why do you think that feeling and being safe is a matter of importance for girls and women during the dating and marriage seasons?

_____
_____
_____
_____

How does the foundational scripture relate to this chapter?

> *{ There's an opportune time to do things, a right time for everything on the earth... A right time to shut up and another to speak up. Ecclesiastes 3:1-7}*

_____
_____
_____
_____
_____
_____
_____
_____

What is emotional intimacy?

_____
_____
_____
_____

When is emotional intimacy healthy and acceptable to our Lord?

_____
_____
_____
_____
_____
_____
_____
_____

When is emotional intimacy unhealthy and unacceptable to Christ?

_____
_____
_____
_____

Read 1 Corinthians 6:12 and 1 Corinthians 10:23. How can these scriptures help young girls, young and older women when confronted with sexually related decisions?

_____
_____
_____
_____

Why do think that the topic of sex and sexual conduct in and outside of marriage makes some Christians uncomfortable?

_____

_____

_____

_____

The Holy Spirit reminds us that nothing is impossible with God and that we can do all things through Christ which strengthens us. That said, why do you think that maintaining virginity and abstinence is difficult for the Child of God?

_____

_____

_____

_____

_____

_____

_____

_____

Share your comments and tweets on how the chapter "Lets Talk About Sex" blessed you on:

https://twitter.com/StephannieBooks
http://www.blogtalkradio.com/stephanniesolomon
Facebook/Conversations With The King Ministries

Chapter Endnotes

1. John 2:4 Jesus said, Is that any of our business, Mother—yours or mine? This isn't my time. Don't push me. (MSG)

2. Matthew 24:14 The Good News about God's kingdom will be preached in all the world, to every nation. Then the end will come. (NCV)

3. Song Of Solomon 2:7 Oh, let me warn you, sisters in Jerusalem, by the gazelles, yes, by all the wild deer: Don't excite love, don't stir it up, until the time is ripe—and you're ready.(MSG)

4. 1 Peter 5:10 And after you suffer for a short time, God, who gives all grace, will make everything right. He will make you strong and support you and keep you from falling. He called you to share in his glory in Christ, a glory that will continue forever.(NCV)

5. Hebrews 2:18 Because he himself suffered when he was tempted, he is able to help those who are being tempted.(NIV)

6. Jude 1:23 Now unto him that is able to keep you from falling, and to present you faultless before the presence of his glory with exceeding joy.(KJV)

7. Romans 8:35 – 39 Can anything separate us from the love Christ has for us? Can troubles or problems or sufferings or hunger or nakedness

or danger or violent death?... nothing above us, nothing below us, nor anything else in the whole world will ever be able to separate us from the love of God that is in Christ Jesus our Lord. (NCV)

8. Proverbs 27:20 Death and Destruction are never satisfied, and neither are human eyes. (NIV)

9. Stephannie Solomon, *Living With The King*: The *King Our Husband,* Bloomington, Indiana, AuthorHouse, 2010, p. 8.

10. Romans 12:1 So brothers and sisters, since God has shown us great mercy, I beg you to offer your lives as a living sacrifice to him. Your offering must be only for God and pleasing to him, which is the spiritual way for you to worship. (NCV)

11. Mark 10:7 For this reason a man shall leave [behind] his father and his mother and be joined to his wife and cleave closely to her permanently, (AMP)

12. Dr. Mike Murdock (2012, July 23). (Twitter Post). Retrieved from https://twitter.com/drmikemurdock.

13. Dr. Lance Watson (2012, June 19). (Twitter Post). Retrieved from https://twitter.com/lancewatson.

14. The Body, *"HIV Epidemic Growing Fastest Among Black Gay and Bisexual Men"*, Center For Disease Control And Prevention (CDC),

http://www.thebody.com/index.html?ic=3001 (August 2011).

15. Science Daily, *"New Way HIV Infects Women Discovered"*,http://www.sciencedaily.com/ releases/2010/04/100408171506.htm (April 2010).

16. Luke 1:37 Nothing is impossible for God!(CEV)

17. Cynthia Gorney, "Too Young to Wed: The Secret World of Child Brides," http://ngm. nationalgeographic.com/2011/06/child-brides/ gorney-text/1, (June 2011).

18. Steven Spielberg, Director, *The Color Purple*, 1985.

19. 1 Corinthians 7:4-5 The marriage bed must be a place of mutuality—the husband seeking to satisfy his wife, the wife seeking to satisfy her husband. Marriage is not a place to "stand up for your rights." Marriage is a decision to serve the other, whether in bed or out. Abstaining from sex is permissible for a period of time if you both agree to it, and if it's for the purposes of prayer and fasting—but only for such times. Then come back together again. Satan has an ingenious way of tempting us when we least expect it. (MSG)

20. Romans 12:1 So brothers and sisters, since God has shown us great mercy, I beg you to offer your lives as a living sacrifice to him. Your offering

must be only for God and pleasing to him, which is the spiritual way for you to worship. (NCV)

21. 2 Corinthians 5:17 Therefore if any man be in Christ, he is a new creature: old things are passed away; behold, all things are become new. (KJV)

22. Leviticus 19:2 Speak to the entire assembly of Israel and say to them: 'Be holy because I, the LORD your God, am holy. (NIV)

23. Pastor A. G. Maclin (2012, July 4). (Twitter Post). Retrieved from https://twitter.com/AGMaclin.

24. Hebrews 13:5 Let your conversation be without covetousness; and be content with such things as ye have: for he hath said, I will never leave thee, nor forsake thee. (KJV)

25. Proverbs 3:6 Listen for God's voice in everything you do, everywhere you go; he's the one who will keep you on track.(MSG)

26. Genesis 2:24 So a man will leave his father and mother and be united with his wife, and the two will become one body. (NCV)

27. Marvin Sapp, "Not The Time, Not The Place", *Grace and Mercy,* 1997, Word, T-5.

28. Ecclesiastes 4:12 And though a man might prevail against him who is alone, two will withstand him. A threefold cord is not quickly broken. (AMP)

29. 2 Samuel 22:31 "As for God, his way is perfect:

The LORD's word is flawless; he shields all who take refuge in him. (NIV)

30. Proverbs 14:12 There is a way that appears to be right, but in the end it leads to death.(NIV)

31. Titus 2:3-5 Guide older women into lives of reverence so they end up as neither gossips nor drunks, but models of goodness. By looking at them, the younger women will know how to love their husbands and children, be virtuous and pure, keep a good house, be good wives. We don't want anyone looking down on God's Message because of their behavior.(MSG)

32. 2 Corinthians 1:4 who comforts us in all our troubles, so that we can comfort those in any trouble with the comfort we ourselves receive from God. (NIV)

33. Matthew 15:14 Let them alone: they be blind leaders of the blind. And if the blind lead the blind, both shall fall into the ditch. (KJV)

34. Stephannie Solomon. *Living With The King: Lead Your Heart.* Bloomington, Indiana, AuthorHouse, 2010. p. 99.

35. 1 Corinthians 10:23 All things are lawful for me, but all things are not expedient: all things are lawful for me, but all things edify not. (KJV)

36. Nehemiah 8:10 Then [Ezra] told them, Go your way, eat the fat, drink the sweet drink, and send portions to him for whom nothing is prepared; for this day is holy to our Lord. And be not

grieved and depressed, for the joy of the Lord is your strength and stronghold. (AMP)

37. Psalm 21:1 The king rejoices in your strength, LORD. How great is his joy in the victories you give!(NIV)

38. Mark 10:9 What therefore God has united (joined together), let not man separate or divide. (AMP)

I Declare

✝

Men shall speak of the might of Your tremendous and terrible
acts, and I will declare Your greatness.(AMP)
Psalm 145:6

Declare Them Innocent

It truly is not worth giving ghosts of the past and people power over our progress, relationships, attitude and more. Even if individuals intentionally engineer events to embarrass, harm or dismiss us, we should not sin with them by holding a grudge. Their manufactured moments of deception may inflame us, but seething over their malicious, immature acts is not God's will for us. There is no gain for us when we inadvertently co-sign with an offender. The wages of sin is death; do not sin with them and die spiritually.[1] Learn to declare those who launch personal attacks innocent. Even if this requires multiple occurrences of this declaration, for our "total wellbeing" it must be done. You and I have the power to do so. Each time we speak this declaration, we are reminded of the freedom that Christ Jesus died and rose for. He died to set the captives free.[2] Choosing not to declare an offender innocent is deciding to be entangled by the yoke of unforgiveness, which is bondage. Also, such a choice reflects a dismissal of Christ's mission to liberate us from the trap of sin.

I once read that a traveling preacher heard the prayer of a child and shared it with others. The child was heard saying, "Forgive us our trash-passes as, we forgive those who pass trash against us."[3] There is nothing like the honesty of a child. Offenses are simply trash. Ladies, we are the Lord's handiwork and He does not make trash. When we are offended, trash, someone's junk, or dysfunction is passed on to us. Since we are not junk we should not embrace the garbage. Because human emotions get tied up in the offense, we tend to get entangled. The more we nurture the thoughts of the offense we create a mental, spiritual and emotional weight. Each weight will work to hinder our growth in the Lord.

Christ gives us grace to endure the brevity and magnitude of weights. Thus, we can all share the same experience, but its duration is laced with the grace of the Lord. God's grace is enough for our individual season of torment. When the season has run its course, we have to release the sting of the offense to the Lord, rather than harvest the memory of every wrong done to us.[4] As I mentioned in the chapter, *Taking Off The Weight*, permit the weight to die and do not interfere with the dying process. Keep in mind that the season of a weighty issue could last minutes, days, weeks, months or even years. There is a season for everything; this includes a season of unforgiveness. Sometimes this season runs longer than it should because we choose to hold a grudge or hold someone hostage to our emotional injury rather than forgive them. In other words, the season of unforgiveness should be a short one rather than a long one once we know what Christ says about it. Once we know His truths, we should act responsively. Notice I mentioned, should. To know what the Lord says to do and to choose not to do it is sin.[5]

Christ instructs us to forgive mainly so that we will be forgiven.[6] Since none of us are perfect and are subject to falling, we must do this so that we can receive mercy. We will all need it. All of us have missed the mark and have the propensity to sin.[7] Knowing that we can and will sin and will need the tender mercies of God, it would behoove us to do the right thing. The right thing is to forgive. Another benefit to forgiving others and even ourselves, is to ready us for genuine service. So many Christians are wasting time and energy because they are just going through the motions of Christian service with an impure heart. This is not operating in Christ's liberty. It is fake and worthless.

Forgiveness releases an offender from guilt and shame, but declaring someone innocent benefits the offended one also. Christ wants the best from us as a witness, worshipper and worker. Truly when we are bound and shackled with debilitating emotions that stem from unforgiveness, we do not serve Christ with gladness and excellence. Our witness is marred and true worship is missing. We also give so much attention to the matter and the person or persons related to it. Living consumed by offenses and offenders is not what Christ meant by standing in the liberty where He set us free. We are people not robots; we have a will to choose. The choice to forgive is weird to the world and sometimes difficult for disciples of Christ. Yet, it is a divine prescription and cure for the saints of God. Christ can use us more and trust us with so much when we are pure in heart, free from holding grudges and forgiving. It is the pure in heart that will see the Lord. [8]We have to want what Christ wants. This is a turning point for all believers.[9] Wiping the slate clean and declaring ourselves and others innocent promotes the wellness of our spiritual, emotional, mental and even physical health.

With the grace and mercy that is extended to us, we should find ourselves extending forgiveness to others. This day we should declare someone innocent. Release them from the guilt, embarrassment, shame, blame, misbehavior and fault whether they own up to the offense or not. Do your spirit good by taking authority over your emotional self. Give yourself relief from resentment, anger, bitterness and sorrow. Empower yourself today as you announce that the slate is clean from an offense. Even if you find yourself forgiving 490 times, forgive until the matter is settled in your spirit.[10] You are not responsible for the poor or wise choices of others, but you are responsible for yourself. Do what is in your power to avoid hurtful scenarios repeating themselves in your life. As much as it depends on you be at peace with yourself and others.[11] Try to be at peace with God.[12] Your growth in Christ depends on you choosing to allow God's perfect peace to flow in your life. This peace will come upon you when you honestly declare yourself and/or someone innocent.

Declare HIS Glory

We state many things in our life time. We assert war on something or someone, broadcast a death, utter praises, certify if one is sane or not, confess our sins, announce our coming out, pronounce people as husbands and wives, profess our faith, pledge allegiance to something, testify for or against, declare something inhabitable, vouch for friends, plead guilt or innocence, say what is on our minds, and state our names. With all that we verbally make known, nothing compares to declarations about the Lord. What we learn of the Lord and all that He says of Himself, we ought to declare.

The heavens declare the glory of God.[13] Since we are created for His glory, we should declare His glory.[14] Stones are willing to cry out in praises of Him if we choose not to.[15] Declaring the ways of God is what we are chosen to do. He is and has been good to us. You and I have to tell others and sometimes remind ourselves of His loyalty.[16] Of the many ways to win souls into the Kingdom of God, telling of His works is so effective.[17] God is worthy to be praised. He gives us many reasons to bless His name and tell of His goodness. He declares amazing things about Himself. He says, "I Am Alpha and Omega, The Beginning and The End, The First and the Last."[18] He also declares that He is The Good Shepherd and so much more.[19] Everything that God says that He is and does, suggest His magnificence, wonder, eminence and sovereignty. He is truly worthy of praise and thanksgiving.

We should give honor to whom honor is due and all honor is due to God.[20] He deserves the glory and the honor. Giving Him His due is good for us and declaring His glory to others is good for them. Declaring His glory is powerful.

It is a reminder to us, the world and Satan that we belong to Christ and He has our back. When we see that everything that the Lord says of Himself is true, we are to agree that He is good and declare that He is wonderful. Declaring these things reflects in whom we have believed. Among other things, it also raises the consciousness of God in those who hear what we declare. It does not matter if the hearers are saved or unsaved; there is the possibility of their heart being opened to God's son when they hear how marvelous He is.[21] As a result to openly declaring the glory of God, we evangelize and witness for Christ.

Announce what the Lord is doing in your life. Declare His righteousness and power. State how His presence has given you joy, confidence and more. Proclaiming His word and works speak life and ultimately gives Him glory. Giving God the glory is one of the many things Kingdom citizens are called to do. It is a way of acknowledging Him, showing Him respect and reverence. In a courtroom we are to rise when the judge enters. In the church we are expected to rise when a Bishop stands to speak. We show respect for our government officials by acknowledging them through titles. God is more than mortal man. Surely we can verbally recognize His authority and make mention of Him. To know of the power of His words and not make mention of it should be uncomfortable.[22] However, once we start to make mention of Him we discover that there are so many wonderful things about Jesus, far too many to declare.[23] Declare what you know anyway. When you do, you will inform, liberate and even destroy that which works against the knowledge of Christ.

Speak over matters, people, including yourself. Now is not the time to be silent. Use your voice. Yes, strong mention of knowing when to hold our tongue is stressed in the chapter "The Art Of Silence"; however, this is not the time to zip it or remain silent on a matter. It is the time to speak, to declare that which the Lord says.[24] Announce in the face of God haters His wonders, ways, words and worth every chance that God gives. This is a great way to give Him glory and honor. I have experienced that declaring the glory of God empowers me when I am confronted with thoughts and activities that war against Him. Such confrontational entities desire the glory for themselves. I am not willing to give them that which is due only to the Lord.

With the authority invested in us we can verbally kill the plans of our opponents. Most times we hear that we should speak words of encouragement, hope, love, and life. We should. However, there are times that we can speak death to those things working against the plan of God. We can arrest in Jesus' name that which comes against the knowledge of Him by simply pronouncing that He is Lord of all. Jesus spoke death over a fig tree.[25] He silenced his haters with declarations of His Lordship and more. Like Christ, our godly declarations will not always be embraced or received with joy, but that are powerful nonetheless. Declarations from the Lord and about the Lord will always give Him glory.

Reflection

Prayer: Lord Jesus your plans, goodness and mercy toward me are many. Remind me Holy Spirit not to take lightly your greatness in my life. I open my heart to you..

_____
_____
_____
_____

Why do you think declaring God's glory and declaring someone innocent is empowering to the one making the declaration?

_____
_____
_____
_____

How do the heavens declare the glory of God? (Psalm 19:1)

_____
_____

Search the scriptures to find at least two things that the Lord declares of Himself. Record the scripture verse, reference and bible version.

_____
_____
_____
_____

How does the foundational scripture relate to this chapter?

{Men shall speak of the might of Your tremendous and terrible acts, and I will declare Your greatness.(AMP) Psalm 145:6}

_____
_____
_____
_____
_____
_____
_____
_____

What four things do you believe that you need to start declaring?

1. _____
2. _____
3. _____
4. _____

Declaring someone innocent is more than trying to forget an offense. Steps are involved in a process of clearing the air and cleansing. List the steps that you have learned are crucial to bringing closure and to moving on in one's life.

_____
_____
_____
_____
_____
_____
_____
_____

The Lord has declared much for and about us. List two scriptures the He declares to us about faith.

_____
_____
_____
_____

List two scriptures that He declares about who we are in Him.

_____
_____

List two scriptures that we can also declare according to scripture, about our health.

_____
_____

Share your comments and tweets on how the chapter "I Declare" blessed you on:

https://twitter.com/StephannieBooks
http://www.blogtalkradio.com/stephanniesolomon
Facebook/Conversations With The King Ministries

Chapter Endnotes

1. Romans 6:23a For the wages of sin is death, but the gift of God is eternal life in Christ Jesus our Lord. (NIV)

2. [2] Luke 4:18 The Lord has put his Spirit in me, because he appointed me to tell the Good News to the poor. He has sent me to tell the captives they are free and to tell the blind that they can see again. — Isaiah 61:1 God sent me to free those who have been treated unfairly — (NCV)

3. Quin Sherrer and Ruthanne Garlock, A Woman's Guide To Spiritual Warfare (Ann Arbor:Servant Publications, 1991) p. 125.

4. Ecclesiastes 3:5 A time to cast away stones, and a time to gather stones together; a time to embrace, and a time to refrain from embracing; (KJV)

5. James 4:17 So any person who knows what is right to do but does not do it, to him it is sin. (AMP)

6. Matthew 6:14 Yes, if you forgive others for their sins, your Father in heaven will also forgive you for your sins. (NCV)

7. Romans 3:23 for all have sinned and fall short of the glory of God, (NIV)

8. Matthew 5:8 Blessed are the pure in heart: for they shall see God. (NIV)

9. Stephannie Solomon, *Conversations With The King: Forgiveness Is Not An Option,* Bloomington, Indiana, AuthorHouse, 1997, 2003, 2009, p. 147.

10. Matthew 18:22 Jesus answered, "I tell you, you must forgive him more than seven times. You must forgive him even if he wrongs you seventy times seven. (NCV)

11. Romans 12:18 If possible, as far as it depends on you, live at peace with everyone. (AMP)

12. 2 Peter 3:14 Dear friends, since you are waiting for this to happen, do your best to be without sin and without fault. Try to be at peace with God. (NCV)

13. Psalm 19:1 The heavens declare the glory of God, and the skies announce what his hands have made. (NCV)

14. Isaiah 43:7 Even every one that is called by my name: for I have created him for my glory, I have formed him; yea, I have made him. (KJV)

15. Luke 19:37 and 40 Right at the crest, where Mount Olives begins its descent, the whole crowd of disciples burst into enthusiastic praise over all the mighty works they had witnessed:... But he said, "If they kept quiet, the stones would do it for them, shouting praise." (MSG)

16. Psalm 89:1 I will always sing about the Lord's

love; I will tell of his loyalty from now on. (NCV)

17. Psalm 107:22 Let them sacrifice thank offerings and tell of his works with songs of joy. (NIV)

18. Revelation 22:13 I am Alpha and Omega, the beginning and the end, the first and the last. (KJV)

19. John 10:11 I am the Good Shepherd. The Good Shepherd risks and lays down His [own] life for the sheep. (AMP)

20. Romans 13:7 Render to all men their dues. [Pay] taxes to whom taxes are due, revenue to whom revenue is due, respect to whom respect is due, and honor to whom honor is due. (AMP)

21. 1 Chronicles 16:24 Declare his glory among the heathen; his marvelous works among all nations. (KJV)

22. Jeremiah 20:9 But if I say, "I will not mention his word or speak anymore in his name," his word is in my heart like a fire, a fire shut up in my bones. I am weary of holding it in; indeed, I cannot. (NIV)

23. Psalm 40:5 Lord my God, you have done many miracles. Your plans for us are many. If I tried to tell them all, there would be too many to count. (NCV)

24. Ecclesiastes 3:7 A time to rend, and a time to sew; a time to keep silence, and a time to speak. (KJV)

25. Matthew 21:`8-20 [*The Withered Fig Tree*]
    Early the next morning Jesus was returning to
    the city. He was hungry. Seeing a lone fig tree
    alongside the road, he approached it anticipating
    a breakfast of figs. When he got to the tree,
    there was nothing but fig leaves. He said, "No
    more figs from this tree—ever!" The fig tree
    withered on the spot, a dry stick. The disciples
    saw it happen. They rubbed their eyes, saying,
    "Did we really see this? A leafy tree one minute,
    a dry sticks the next?" (MSG)

Super Models

✠

But mostly, show them all this by doing it yourself, incorruptible in your teaching, your words solid and sane. Then anyone who is dead set against us, when he finds nothing weird or misguided, might eventually come around.(MSG)
Titus 2:7-8

The It Factor

The Perfect One, Jesus Christ calls us to imitate Him.[1] The imperfect apostle Paul begged disciples like us to follow him.[2] So who are we imitating if one model is perfect and the other is not? We are striving to be like Christ so that we will be presented faultless before God our Father.[3] Christ says that we can do "all" things through Him which strengthens us. With His Spirit in us which raised Him from the dead, we can live godly and win. For the times that we fall, we can still win. Like Paul, practicing the ways of Christ, we too can fight the good fight and win. A lifestyle of confession and repentance will certainly help us triumph in all things. Our lives can become a wonderful reflection and representation of God at work in us. We have what it takes to model the God way.

When those who do not know God observe us, they should see a stance for righteousness, a turn away from sin and a pose that waits on the Lord. Our godly convictions are weird to them. The world and carnal Christians wonder what is it that makes us tick and how is it that we do what we do. Some are so curious and hateful of what the Lord has put in us to survive and thrive that they will go through unusual lengths to find out what motivates us in Jesus. I have observed haters attempt to form relationships with individuals who are close to those they hate, just to learn what makes their enemy happy. They are not comfortable with the Woman of God so they attempt to form superficial relationships with people around the Woman of God. This is sad, conniving, manipulative, but it is true.

There is something about Women of Faith that is not easily read or seen by those who do not know God. Whether admired or despised, these models for Christ possess and display something that is peculiar to those who reject the Lord. Those who disapprove of the expected lifestyle of a Christian do not understand that for women who are sold out for Christ their choices are always rooted in the resurrection of Jesus Christ. Everything that Women of God model before the world, centers around the belief that Jesus died for the world's sins and rose Himself up from the grave and lives, interceding on our behalf daily. It is in Him that these women live. The biblical standards that these appointed models live by, creates an appeal that sets them apart from others. They are imperfect, yet chosen. They are the Lord's "super models."

Models of this caliber draw both haters and helpers because they have chosen to live an exemplary life in Christ Jesus. This lifestyle encompasses human imperfection, yet the discerning eye will see characteristics of Christ Jesus. Such godly attributes are factors that qualify a woman to be called Woman Of God. She is a role model who shows how to live in every aspect of her life. What the Lord has given her and allowed to enter into her space, through Him, she works. She works what she has. Because of her convictions, girls and women embrace her example for living. Even men and boys grow to admire the way that she embraces her femininity and godly favor.

Christ's super models are not models that have that indescribable something which makes them special. The discerning eye sees that what they possess is definable. Their successes in Christ outweigh their losses. The "it factor" at some point becomes known. Compassion could be the factor that draws people to God's Woman. Maybe it is diligence, tenacity, integrity, or fortitude that sets her apart and sets her up for attraction and interaction. Unlike the world who celebritizes people with the "it factor", God's super models graciously serve and worship Him with that special something. He gets the glory, not them. His name, words and ways are made known and lifted high in all the earth through their graceful use of their God given abilities. The yardstick by which one measures and examines their "it" factor should be the Word of God, for these women speak and live all of God's Word. What they do is confirmed in God's Word. Their choices are driven and proven by godly wisdom. As mentioned in the chapter "The Art Of Silence", wisdom is justified, proven to be right by what it does (Luke 7:35).

Grace And The Other Woman

For God's Woman, the "it" factor is the supernatural ability to do something for Christ with ease. Other women can mimic "it", but fail at doing it with the grace and anointing that God has sanctioned the super model to do. This anointing, grace and spiritual gift is attractive. The Lord has made the "it" factor beautiful and it draws attention from haters and helpers. Everyone is not pleased with the Lord's sovereignty to select who He wants to do what He wants. This displeasure towards the Lord and His chosen servants create a porthole for Satan to enter.[4] Know that availing oneself to be used of Satan to harass or harm women in Christ is never a wise choice and if opted will have dire consequences.

There are many forms of taunting and provocation that women inflict upon other women. The reasons are never of God and they are birthed out of ignorance, fear, jealousy and envy. God's super models have to resist the temptation to go low like their contenders. We are to rise and remain above the godlessness. Only the Lord can take super models to that height or place. Many wives are scoffed by women who have lowered their standards to engage in clandestine and open emotional and/or sexual relations with their husbands. Realistically it takes two to tangle; however, we are all responsible for evaluating our actions.[5] Society has labeled women who agree to relations with a married man as the other woman. She is the other interest of a husband and is aware of what she is doing. Yet, like all sinners, she is redeemable too. What the wife or fiancée needs to focus on is her relationship with Christ in the midst of turmoil, lunacy and sorrow. In all of this the Lord still wants someone to exemplify holiness while going through hell. The fight is on because the enemies of Christ want to destroy the witness of hope, health and healing in Christ Jesus. The weight and sting of the affair destroys so much, yet the Spirit of the Lord is so able to do "exceeding abundantly" above all that we ask or think.

Wives and fiancées are not responsible for their husband's or fiancé's lack of character or self-control. Neither are they the reason for him acting on unholy thoughts. What women of God have to be ready to embrace is that they may be required to be the Lord's conduit that leads someone to a place in Christ that changes their life forever. The targeted person may be an offender, partaker, supporter or eyewitness to the affair. The real fight is on. This is the fight that Satan does not want won or acknowledged. There is more at stake than personal feelings, pain and materialism. Truly no weapon forged against the servant of God has power to prevail. Therefore, any wife or wife to be, who finds herself in this sick and dark place, has to also find it within herself to rejoice in knowing that she has been chosen by the Heavenly Father to handle something that is winnable because the Lord has given her the grace to win. Every Child of God has what it takes to win and win big. Moreover, it is the "it" that the Lord has deposited into His servant that has trouble and testimony vying for victory.

If the "other woman" comes against the servant of Christ, she will not prosper, for the "it" that she covets and envies will condemn her.[6] The super model in Christ will condemn the other woman's words and works.[5] The other woman is no match for what the Lord has ordained. She lacks the wisdom, competence, style, class, and grace to win in Christ this battle, whereas super models in Jesus are anointed and appointed to win in the messiest of trials. They are overcomers. The good wife, the godly woman has confidence in the Lord. Self-confidence in herself is good, but it is not the determinate that makes her prosper in God. She knows this. Her focus is not on herself, the other woman, or others. Rather she looks to Christ for everything. The "it factor" that God gave her involves confidence and expectation in God alone, for He gives the self-confidence, strength and joy to do whatever the mission is called for. Modeling consistently with the mindset to rely on God will create super models who are set apart. It is this setting apart that reveals the grace of God at work, condemns nay sayers and shuts the mouths of mockers. Others will call her blessed and willingly follow her example. Whoever the enemy has designated to use as the other woman will surrender to the power of Christ at work in God's chosen vessel. In secret they will come for forgiveness and in fear they will run. The "it" factor has power. It draws and dominates the enemies of our Christ. Thus, work the "it" divinely given. It was not given to lie dormant and unused. In the right season it shall come forth and give God all of the glory that He alone desires and deserves.

Parenting 101

The "it factor" will enable us to do what has to be done. It will equip us to pursue and conquer. It will do so much including encouraging others to trust the Lord Jesus for direction. We need divine direction for every aspect of life. One area in particular that no one should oust the help of God in is parenting. Only the Lord's guidelines for parents work. They work because He is the Beginning and the End, as well as the All Knowing God. He knew our children before they were formed in the womb.[7] Many children, especially young children, do not see parents as human. So many feel that parents are insensitive and cannot relate to any current issues. Nonetheless, parents are people too. They make mistakes. Parents do not always get it right. Many people have become parents with poor or no training. However, parents should be continual learners. We should always be learning as we grow. Just as I mentioned in an earlier chapter that marriage is not for wimps, parenting is not for wimps either. Do not have children if you are not willing to learn to become a parent.

One aspect of parenting is learning to say, "I am sorry". We have to be big enough to apologize to our children when our choices have offended or traumatized them. It will go a long way and bless us when we and our children are older and in need of one another. There are cultures that believe the mantra, "Do as I say, not as I do". Well what we model before our children is what most of them will end up doing even when they do not want to. Many children promise themselves not to repeat the sins of the mother or father, yet statistics prove that many will indulge in those same revolting habits and sins. Sadly many people who are addicted to something witnessed the life of an addict through their parents. When I say addict, I am referring to someone who relies on a habit, activity or substance to experience temporary satisfaction. Some forms of addictions are shopping, sex, drugs, alcohol, gambling, food, viewing pornography, playing video games, exercise, using the computer, internet or social media.

There is another mantra that many individuals can relate to and that is "I brought you in this world and I'll take you out". Now that sounds like someone who is on a serious power trip. Here is a reality check for all. The Lord and the Lord alone is responsible for any of us being here. Our times are in His hands.[8] He has fearfully and wonderfully made us, not our parents (Psalm 139:14) When we say things to our children we should be mindful of the possible results. Hopefully, even in anger, we want to speak words that will not harm or hinder the child in the present or the future. We are accountable for our words.[9] If we are not careful, we can provoke our children to anger rather than admiration for the things of God. Often we hear and read how children are to obey their parents and they should. However, the scriptures reveal that just as children should submit to their parents, parents are to submit to their children, not provoking them to anger.[10] To do so, is to break their spirit, discouraging them rather than encouraging them.[11]

As a parent we are to model through word and deed that which we expect from our children. In addition, correction from the parent on the front end will not be an excuse or embarrassment later. Does this mean that when a child executes poor choices that the parents or guardians are always at fault? Absolutely not. In retrospect there are some personal choices that have absolutely nothing to do with how one was parented. However, there will be some behaviors children exhibit that parents must take responsibility for. Maybe a parent's absence or failure to lovingly communicate created emotional issues or walls of distrust. Possibly silence on abuse established self-destructive behaviors. Could it be that a parent preferred one child over another? There may have been instances where the parent incited arguments among the siblings, stepping aside watching violence and hostility that he/she was the very cause of. The list can go on. Parents have to be honest and take responsibility for matters of the heart that they have contributed to. School, neighborhood and other aspects of life contribute to experiences and perceptions that children develop. However, parents are the first community network that children experience. How we love on our children or fail to love on them will have a tremendous impact on how they perceive themselves and others.

Parents are watched by their offspring more than they know. Children see their parents' faults and many are forgiving and resilient. However, forgiveness and resiliency does not guarantee the dismissal of the effects parental choices have on a child. The results may not appear until they begin dating or some other pivotal time in their life. Moving beyond adversity with parents does not mean that total healing has occurred in a child. Only the intervention of the Lord can ensure that the child is educated enough not to repeat egregious offenses that were done to them. Yet, when we become Children of God, all things work together for the good of those who love God. This scripture is not applicable for everyone, only those who love God. We know that we love God when we obey all that He has to say to us.[12]

Mistakes in parenting happen. The potential for a parental crisis is always around the bend. There are no perfect parents because there are no perfect people. However, when holes and walls are created in the relationship between parent and child, the Lord can heal the tares and dry the tears. Still mothers and fathers have to take responsibility for the scars that they created in their child's life. Saying that one did the best that they could is not always good enough or an excuse. Accept and acknowledge wrong doing that created problems for the children. Repent and then move forward. To err is human, to repent divine, to persist in ways of selfishness, is devilish.[13] There are parents who do not want to admit that they wounded their child emotionally, psychologically, sexually, or physically because of their poor choices and pride. Many do not see how their behaviors contribute to their child's poor self-image, emotional, sexual, physical and mental issues. Acknowledging one's role in an offspring's troubles is a start. Christ is available to heal and deliver all involved. Whether group and/or individual therapy is a part of the healing process, salvation is available for all family members.

Parenting can be difficult. Still, when done correctly, it is a rewarding responsibility. Indeed parenting has its challenges, but challenges do not mean that quitting on our children is an option. Parents have to see their children in their future living well. They have to see themselves beyond the present also living in the promises of God. Our perceptions of this role and gift will be revealed in our parenting choices. Sense this read is geared to women, I believe that mothers want to be virtuous. Even though many mothers do not know how to be virtuous in accordance to the way of the Lord, many want to love their children unconditionally and desire that their children love and respect them. I know that there are mental issues with many mothers, but I believe that many mothers want their children to call them blessed in spite of their past mistakes and current hurdles. I choose to believe that many mothers want their children and their children's children in their lives. Yet, to be in your children's memories tomorrow, you have to be in their lives today.[14]

Many mothers have unknowingly practiced generational dysfunctions on their daughters and sons, but Christ declares that He has come to set us free.[15] Choosing to raise our children in the admonition of the Lord is one way to believe God for protection, provision and pardon. I am not referring to sending your child to church with the hope that such an activity will correct negative behavior and save their souls. I am referring to living godly before your child, modeling righteousness and teaching them through behavior and conversation the ways of Christ Jesus. Such examples would be teaching them how to love, pray, forgive, resist peer pressure, serve the Lord, stand during opposition, as well as exercising patience, tenacity, wisdom, integrity, diligence and faithfulness. These principles should be biblical teachings, not slogans, old wives tales, fables, sayings passed down through the family or positive thinking.

Children should see and hear mothers praying to Christ. We should be so inclined to learn about the postures of prayers and teach these postures to our children. Making time to share in the word together is essential. How can we expect our youth and young people to refer to something that they have no reference to, model for, or tools to use? Give them something good and solid to take with them. The world is no friend to God's grace; thus, our children need to be taught how to fight with the Lord's armor and weaponry that is mighty through God. They should know how to declare the Word of God appropriately, denounce any form of negativity with the name and blood of Jesus Christ. Their successes depend on consistent application of each one of these. Witnessing a parent praying, reading the bible, serving the Lord joyfully, and pleading the blood of Jesus is a powerful tool. Memories of such encounters and the victorious results speak volumes to a growing child. This is training a child in the way that he/she should go.[16] They learn by doing and what they witnessed their parents do. As resilient as many children are, they do not forget. They observe how mothers love or refuse to love themselves, their own siblings and parents, their lovers, husbands, neighbors and others. Thus, mothers should strongly consider how they live before their children. Living to leave a legacy worthy of honor should be a goal.

For the mothers who have contributed to confusion and considerable misgivings in their children's lives, the love of Christ is available for forgiveness. The grace of God is extended for repentance. Even if others insist on conjuring up unpleasant memories of misdeeds done to children, redemption is near. Ill-equipped and unloving mothers are redeemable too. The love of God is available to all. It is the wise woman; however, who chooses to trust in God's love. If she parents, she can trust that love to make her a fine example, worthy of followship. Live the life that figuratively says, 'I can show you better than I can tell you". Super mothers, super moms, show and maybe tell how to walk before the Lord. Her life will reflect a love for God which positively influences and impacts the development of her children, who eventually call her blessed.

Long Suffering

Christians are called to model Christ in every way. So often we choose to decide which parts of the bible to agree with and/or which words from God to believe and live by.[17] Although, we are free to refuse, we are invited to heed Ephesians 5:1 which tells us to imitate Christ, Son of the Living God. One characteristic of Christ and a feature of His co-laborers is long suffering. Often used interchangeably with patience, it surpasses waiting. It means long and patient endurance of a hardship, sickness or provocation. In my opinion, like the godly attributes humility, patience, love, faith, and discipline, there seems to be an absence of this godly trait in many of the Lord's people. Like the aforementioned qualities, it works to define those who worship the Lord in spirit and in truth.[18]

In an age where things are desired and distributed quick, fast and in a hurry, it has become difficult for many Christians to strip themselves from impatience, anxiousness, impulsiveness and restlessness. Living like the world, there are moments when Children of God want the Lord to move on their behalf without delay. Yet, in Christ, delay does not mean denial. The Lord is true to His word. He is attentive to every aspect of our lives. He will hear and answer our prayers; He will comfort, protect and provide for us. The Lord our God will finish what He started in our lives and never abandon us. God is on our side; however, this does not mean that we will get what we want from God always or get it in the time frame that we have set. His ways truly are unlike what we think they should be.[19]

God is long suffering towards us.[20] Often we hear talk of how the Lord is insensitive towards the evil and suffering of mankind. Yet, do we think of how long suffering He is towards each of us? Humanity tends to place more emphasis on being receivers from what the Lord can give us rather than givers to the Lord. We have to be reminded that we are not our own.[21] Through the blood of Christ Jesus our Lord, we have been bought with a price not to live soaking up physical wealth from the Lord, but rather to live in and for Him; getting strength, anointing and gifts from Him in order to be a blessing to the world.[22]

God is able to keep us in any circumstance. He is able to cloth us with His righteousness that while we are in the thick of it we wear our assigned suffering well.[23]

Yes suffering is assigned by God for each of us. It brings forth the true character of Christ. God tries us. Like Job, when He is finished His perfect work in us, we will pass inspection with flying colors.[24] Truly as a Child of God we do not have to wear our suffering or issues of the heart on our sleeves. Only the Lord has a way of making us look as though we have not endured the pain and trouble that we have encountered. Cosmetics do not get the credit for God's make-over.

Suffering in and of itself is one thing. Having to suffer long is quite another. Thus, endurance to continue in mess until the Lord releases us is essential for an incomparable breakthrough. Going through is necessary for the godly results of passing God's test. There is a flip to the mess and we have got to believe that Christ will give us what it takes to endure, persevere and live to enjoy what is on the other side of the challenge. We have to desire to not just wanting to see what is on the other side of a problem, but we should also desire to live in what is on the other side of it. The enemies of Christ will work fervently to tempt us to give in and walk away from trusting God for deliverance. Opponents of

Christ do not want us to experience the fulfillment of God's promises. Still be encouraged. Remember we are on God's mind, His radar. We are not forgotten. Although tempting, do not believe the report of anyone who tells us that it is better to trust in ourselves, common sense or anything other than God. It is easier to quit than to pursue with hardship. However, that which is easy is not always what is best for our lives or line up with the route to our purpose. Suffering long seems the unlikely route to our purpose, destiny and a new level in Jesus. Yet, often this is the way of choice from our All Knowing and All Wise Heavenly Father. There is no other route to get to where He desires us to be.

The Lord's report to stand, wait on Him, trust and believe Him is a living report from Him. Suffering will work for our good and take us as well as those who we model before to a better place psychologically, spiritually, emotionally and oft times physically. Christ's suffering was not in vain and neither will ours be when we rely totally on Him during periods of long suffering. He suffered and won. So can we. Modeling Christ in every way is possible. He will show us how to endure the test because we can do all things, not some things, through Him, which give us strength. People are looking to see if victories are possible in every kind of trial. Yes, we can model the results before them. We model by faith in God, not in fear or feelings, for it will be our love for God and our faith in God that enables us to suffer long and win.

Mirror, Mirror

In the 1700's German brothers Jacob and Wilhelm Grimm created a collection of well-known folk and fairytales which were translated into English in 1820. Many of these stories have become household names because of the animated versions of them created by Walt Disney. One story in particular is Snow White and the Seven Dwarfs. The antagonist in this fairytale is a wicked queen who periodically asks a magical mirror who is the fairest female in the kingdom. At the time in which the story was written fair or pale in complexion was equivalent to being rated a 10 on today's beauty scale. The implication was that if a female was fair, she was pleasing in appearance or physically attractive. The evil queen from the fairytale envied any female who was naturally attractive. Dissatisfied with her own appearance, she was always chasing the next concoction to enhance her outer self.

Although this character exists in a make believe story, her negative thoughts of herself exist in reality. The queen had a constant need to continually hear that she was the fairest in the land. She continually sought out her rivals while coveting what they possessed. What an example of an unfulfilled life. Her use of wickedness to expose and eradicate her clueless competitors also revealed the lack of godliness in her heart. The counter to such a superficial life is to embrace godliness with contentment.[25] The combination of the two will bless any life immensely.

Looking at the woman in the mirror should be a good thing, especially when the purpose is for self- improvement. The reflection of one's self should cause introspect and retrospect that lead to a change in thinking as well as behaviors. The queen in the original story of Snow White did not use the mirror for this purpose. Instead, she wanted the mirror to cosign onto what she adored about herself; to feed her insecurity. Our life is no fairy tale, but like the queen, many women look in mirrors hoping to see something that agrees with a false image of themselves. The truth is that the reflection ought to cause self-examination which is to lead to our betterment. Christ says that we should test and examine our motives and our conduct.[26] This is a prescription as well as a preventive measure for pride and self- aggrandizement. Seeing and knowing that we are imperfect beings, a desire for inner change should be created during moments of self-reflection. Thus, confession and repentance should always be on the horizon.

When we change inwardly we began to see what really matters. We see how ill our thoughts are and how they need divine guidance. Real inner change reveals who God is, how He operates and why we need Him. Godly transformation exposes the matters that we should address and those that need to be laid aside. Ladies through true change Christ will show us where there is covetousness. When we covet something that belongs to someone else, generally envy and jealousy are nearby. Our God does not want us to live manipulated and guided by such spirits. He does not desire that we live like the queen in Snow White. Rather He desires that we live as His worshippers, witnesses and warriors.

We really should not spend time coveting anything that another sister has. If what she has is for us, God can give it to us. Keep in mind; however, that even if we share the same gift, the way in which the Lord chooses to use us and our gifts will differ. Grow and prosper where you are and with what you have. Chasing after anything to make us like someone else minimizes and ignores the worth of the precious uniqueness in which we have been wonderfully created. Spending time coveting what does not belong to us keeps us from our position to bless and be blessed. Just as we all have divine assignments, we have divine stations. There are specific places where we are supposed to be at specific times for specific purposes.

Queen Esther was aware of this. She knew that her positioning, her station and her purpose were God ordained.[24] My concern is that many women have not recognized their stations; where they are called to work it out for Christ. There is a portion of God's peculiar women who have rejected their appointed placement. They are busy looking at what someone else is doing or has. Mind your business may sound trite, but we have business for God to do and we need to be about it now.[27] As witnesses for God, our business is really God's business. Coveting competes with the Lord's business. The Lord gives us a forum or forums to witness and share the good news. We can miss the work, witness or opportunity simply by being out of position. Thus, it is so important to stay focused, stay the course and flow in the wisdom of God.

Moreover, longing for someone or something to complete us is an affront to God. He really is our sufficiency and He is more than enough. Christ was sent to make us whole and complete.[28] A lie of this world tells us that people or things make us complete. This is contradictory to the words of our Lord. We do not have another half walking around somewhere. Think about this. Christ promised to complete in us what He started and told us that we are complete in Him. He does not lie.[27] Neither does Christ need people to complete us; He does. This misunderstanding of completeness is one of several reasons why many women possess low self-worth because they have no one to date or marry. I am in no way endorsing living so independent of a man that there is no room for a male mate. I am endorsing that women become focused and centered on becoming whole or complete individuals so that their choices of men do not cause regret and that they do not become obviously needy for the acceptance of people rather than God. We need God.

One other area that I would like to address when seeking sincere self-reflection is alliance; there should be an awareness of who we bring to our reflection party. Be careful not to launch a band wagon for those who agree with our sin and partake in our misconduct. These are unhealthy alliances and relationships regardless, of who the individuals are. We are called and chosen to model for Christ with excellence. Trying to emulate the Master of Light with dark attachments is unacceptable. Our plan will fail. Subpar efforts are also unacceptable. Christ gave His best and has left for us means for us to give Him the best. Thus, watch the company that is kept.[29] Anyone who cosigns onto our dysfunctions and sin is not a friend and surely does not have our best interest.

Reflection

Prayer: Lord God I know that I am not perfect. What areas of my life do you want me to attend to so that I am an exemplary model for Christ? After reading...

_____
_____
_____
_____

Since God has promised never to leave us, does it really matter if we walk away from the position and station that He has assigned for us? Explain.

_____
_____
_____
_____

Of the eight scriptures noted in the section "Long Suffering", which one tugs at your heart the most at this time? Why?

_____
_____
_____
_____

What word comes to mind when you think of the "it" factor for a Woman of God?

_____

List at least three traits that make for a godly parent. Explain.

_____
_____
_____
_____
_____
_____
_____
_____

The fairytale question "Mirror mirror on the wall who is the fairest of them all?" signifies what deficiencies in the person asking?

_____
_____
_____
_____
_____
_____
_____
_____
_____
_____

God is great. His Spirit lives within Christians and His son Jesus Christ declared that His followers would do what He did as well as greater things. We can be super mothers, super workers, super wives, super writers, super cleaners, super cooks, super examples and more.

List three areas in your life where you desire to be a super model for Christ.

_____

_____

_____

_____

How does the foundational scripture relate to this chapter?

{ But mostly, show them all this by doing it yourself,
incorruptible in your teaching, your words solid and sane. Then
anyone who is dead set against us, when he finds nothing weird
or misguided, might eventually come around. Titus 2:7-8}

_____

_____

_____

_____

_____

_____

_____

_____

From your reading, how are patience and long suffering different?

_____

_____

_____

_____

_____

_____

_____

_____

How are these two similar?

_____
_____
_____
_____

How can servants of God benefit from self-reflection?

_____
_____
_____
_____

Read and meditate on Galatians 6:4. How is this scripture a prescription for living?

_____
_____
_____
_____
_____
_____

How can Christian mothers work to raise children who reflect godly parenting?

_____
_____
_____
_____
_____
_____
_____

Why is self-reflection good?

_____

_____

_____

_____

Because we are fearfully and wonderfully made, we all have an "it factor". Have you discovered yours? If so, what is it? If not, what are you doing to discover it?

_____

_____

_____

_____

Share your comments and tweets on how the chapter "Super Models" blessed you on:

https://twitter.com/StephannieBooks
http://www.blogtalkradio.com/stephanniesolomon
Facebook/Conversations With The King Ministries

Chapter Endnotes

1. Ephesians 5:1 Therefore be imitators of God [copy Him and follow His example], as well-beloved children [imitate their father]. (AMP)

2. 1 Corinthians 4:16 So I urge and implore you, be imitators of me. (AMP)

3. Colossians 1:22 Yet now has [Christ, the Messiah] reconciled [you to God] in the body of His flesh through death, in order to present you holy and faultless and irreproachable in His [the Father's] presence. (AMP)

4. John 13:27 And after the sop Satan entered into him. Then said Jesus unto him, That thou doest, do quickly. (KJV)

5. Galatians 6:4 But let every person carefully scrutinize and examine and test his own conduct and his own work. He can then have the personal satisfaction and joy of doing something commendable [in itself alone] without [resorting to] boastful comparison with his neighbor. (AMP)

6. Isaiah 54:17 So no weapon that is used against you will defeat you. You will show that those who speak against you are wrong. These are the good things my servants receive. Their victory comes from me," says the Lord. (NCV)

7. Jeremiah 1:5 Before I formed you in the womb I knew you, before you were born I set you apart; I appointed you as a prophet to the nations. (NIV)

8. Psalm 31:15 My times are in Your hands; deliver me from the hands of my foes and those who pursue me and persecute me. (AMP)

9. Matthew 12:37 For by your words you will be justified *and* acquitted, and by your words you will be condemned *and* sentenced. (AMP)

10. Ephesians 6:4 And, ye fathers, provoke not your children to wrath: but bring them up in the nurture and admonition of the Lord. (KJV)

11. Colossians 3:21 Fathers, do not provoke or irritate or fret your children [do not be hard on them or harass them], lest they become discouraged and sullen and morose and feel inferior and frustrated. [Do not break their spirit.] (AMP)

12. 1 John 5:1-3 Every person who believes that Jesus is, in fact, the Messiah, is God-begotten. If we love the One who conceives the child, we'll surely love the child who was conceived. The reality test on whether or not we love God's children is this: Do we love God? Do we keep his commands? The proof that we love God comes when we keep his commandments and they are not at all troublesome. (MSG)

13. The Electric Ben Franklin, Independence Hall Association, http://www.ushistory.org/franklin/quotable/index.htm,ushistory.org, 1995.

14. Serita Jakes (2012, September 2). (Twitter Post). Retrieved from https://twitter.com/FirstLadyJakes.

15. Isaiah 49:8-9 God also says: "When the time's

ripe, I answer you. When victory's due, I help you. I form you and use you to reconnect the people with me, To put the land in order, to resettle families on the ruined properties. I tell prisoners, 'Come on out. You're free!' (MSG)

16. Proverbs 22:6 Train up a child in the way he should go: and when he is old, he will not depart from it. (KJV)

17. Hebrews 11:1 Now faith is confidence in what we hope for and assurance about what we do not see. Now faith is confidence in what we hope for and assurance about what we do not see. (NIV)

18. John 4:23 But the hour cometh, and now is, when the true worshippers shall worship the Father in spirit and in truth: for the Father seeketh such to worship him. (KJV)

19. Isaiah 55:8 The Lord says, "My thoughts are not like your thoughts. Your ways are not like my ways. (NCV)

20. Psalm 86:15 But thou, O Lord, art a God full of compassion, and gracious, long suffering, and plenteous in mercy and truth. (KJV)

21. 1 Corinthians 6:19 Do you not know that your bodies are temples of the Holy Spirit, who is in you, whom you have received from God? You are not your own, (NIV)

22. 1 Corinthians 6:20 For ye are bought with a price: therefore glorify God in your body, and in your spirit, which are God's. (KJV)

23. Stephannie Solomon. *Conversations With The King: You Wear It Well.* Bloomongton, Indiana, AuthorHouse, 1997, 2003, 2009, pp.67-72.

24. Job 23:10 But God knows the way that I take, and when he has tested me, I will come out like gold. (NCV)

25. 1 Timothy 6:6 [And it is, indeed, a source of immense profit, for] godliness accompanied with contentment (that contentment which is a sense of inward sufficiency) is great *and* abundant gain. (AMP)

26. Galatians 6:4 But let every person carefully scrutinize and examine and test his own conduct and his own work. He can then have the personal satisfaction and joy of doing something commendable [in itself alone] without [resorting to] boastful comparison with his neighbor. (AMP)

27. Esther 4:14 For if you remain silent at this time, relief and deliverance for the Jews will arise from another place, but you and your father's family will perish. And who knows but that you have come to your royal position for such a time as this? (NIV)

28. Stephannie Solomon. *Conversations With The King: Mind Your Business.* Bloomongton, Indiana, AuthorHouse, 1997, 2003, 2009, pp. 189-206.

29. Colossians 2:10 And ye are complete in him, which is the head of all principality and power: (KJV)

He's Just That In To You

✝

This is how much God loved the world: He gave his Son, his one and only Son. And this is why: so that no one need be destroyed; by believing in him, anyone can have a whole and lasting life. (MSG)
John 3:16

Happy Ever After

Unlike many people, the Lord is not afraid of intimacy. He desires it. Intimacy is not the same as commitment. The Lord is so in to us that He can and will do both. He also desires both from us. As the intimate God, He has no problem with touching us and wanting to be touched by us. He is just that in to us. When we are in His presence there is fullness of joy.[1] Communicating with us is not an issue with the Lord either. He wants to talk to us and wants us to talk to Him.[2] The Lord is a great listener.[3] Our God is all about building a loving, honest and trusting relationship with us. He is as real and authentic as His word. Since He does not lie, His word is bond. His ways of loving on us are far from what any person could give; they are perfect.

Our Groom Jesus is so in to us ladies that when He vows to support, encourage and protect us, He does just that. We are called to fellowship with and follow someone who is so faithful.[4] He does not switch gears and decide before or during the relationship to bow out for any reason. Our vices and sinful human attributes are grounds for Him to divorce us at any time, but Christ remains faithful to us and to what He has started within us.[5] He says what He means and He means what He says. He vows to love us with an everlasting love.[6] His covenant with us is everlasting.[7] We can bank on Him always being near. Our Groom, Our Husband, Our Christ is so in to us that even as He loves on others, there is no partiality towards us. He sees us, knows us and desires that we see and know Him. He loved us before we knew Him and He will love us forever.

Life with Christ is no fairytale, but He is our prince, Prince of Peace. Our journey with Him is not perfect, but every day with Him is sweeter than the day before. There is fulfillment in loving on Him and having Him love on us. Absolutely nothing can separate us from His matchless love.[8] What He got started within us, He plans to complete.[9] In human marriages, there are a myriad of things that can separate the bride from her groom, which includes death. However, our marriage to Christ is forever even if death is allowed to touch the body of the bride. To be absent from the body is to be present with the Lord.[10] In this wonderful relationship with the Lord there is guaranteed togetherness. While we are on earth, Christ has promised never to abandon us.[11] Eternal life with Him is assured.[12] As the perfect Husband, He has prepared residency, a home, for His Bride in heaven.[13] In the tune of the hit song "What a Man" by Salt N Pepa, we can sing, What a God, what a God, what a mighty good God. He's a mighty mighty good God. Yes He is.

He Only Has Eyes For You

Christ is in to us and He wants the world to know it. He wants us, His people, to know it. We can tell that He is in to us because He cares for what He has created and that which is affiliated with Him.[14] A good husband cares for his wife and wants others to know it. She is a reflection of his self-worth. He will not want her to dress in a way that is disgusting or that debases her. What she wears and drives may not be the latest in fashion and fad, but her clothes, hair and car will be well kept. If he cannot clean her car, he will make sure that it gets clean. He will creatively come up with ways to show off her beauty and grace which attracted him to her. It is a sad state of affairs when a husband allows his wife to look her worst and he is comfortable with it.

The God in whom we serve wants only the best for us. He has made us, so He knows what is in each of us that is of great worth. He is proud of us and wants others to know that we are His and that He is our God. Other than caring for us and hearing us, there are several other ways that prove that Our Groom, our Husband, our God is in to us. One that is close to my heart is that He sees us.[15] We are not an ignored creation of God or an afterthought. He sees the suffering, maliciousness, greed, idolatry, perversion and He sees those who love Him. In His matchless and marvelous way He lets us know that He sees us. In His time He will make beautiful that which is hideous in our lives.[16] According to His plan, He will finish what He started.[17] He sees our struggles and sorrows. He also sees our triumphs and our tomorrows. He is attentive because He is that in to us.

Our God sees all and cares.[18] His eye is on the sparrow, yet we should know that He watches over us even more.[19] We are cherished above the birds of the air; we are the apple of His eye.[20] Jesus, the lover of our soul is just so in to us. We can find grace in His eyes, for He is not watching us with a desire to see us fail.[21] Christ is rooting for our successes in Him. We cannot fly under the radar with Him because He is the God who sees us and all that we do. Like a loving and attentive parent, He is involved in His children's lives. We can count on Him showing up. That said, no pain, longing or dream goes unnoticed and unaddressed by Him when we commit them to Him. He will deal with our matters because He is looking for women to use.[22]

In a nutshell our continued hope in Christ will bring on the blessed results. There is blessed assurance knowing that His eyes are on us.[23] We are special to Him and His look towards us means that He is definitely interested in us. With redemption and grace, He loves us all enough to form a relationship that spans time and proceeds to eternity. He is willing to go the long haul and be what we need Him to be because He is that into us.

Reflections

Prayer: Holy Spirit your Word says that you have your eyes on every man and woman. You don't miss a trick. Thank you for loving me so much. How can…..

I show more love to you.
- I love talking to You
- I love hearing from you
- I love being with you
- I love fellowshipping with others

The Lord is about building relationships with us. Explain how the following three scriptures support this fact.

Jeremiah 29:12 "When you call on me, when you come and pray to me, I'll listen."

The Lord wants us to seek Him
He already knows us we need
to call on Him. He is openly and
ready to take us in and hear us.

Jeremiah 31:3 The LORD appeared to us in the past, saying: "I have loved you with an everlasting love; I have drawn you with unfailing kindness."

He has always been there Regardless of how we act or acted.

Jeremiah 33:3 "Call to me and I will answer you and tell you great and unsearchable things you do not know."

Reach out to Him. He will renew your mind. Such things will take place that you won't nothing else to say but ONLY GOD!!

Why do you think that Christians should believe in the grace of God?

Because God does things for us that he really I mean Really don't have to do.

Name at least five things that the Lord does differently than men in showing just how into us He is?

1. Provides
2. don't lie
3. heals
4. love me in spite of
5. forgives

How does the foundational scripture relate to this chapter?

{ This is how much God loved the world: He gave his Son, his one and only Son. And this is why: so that no one need be destroyed; by believing in him, anyone can have a whole and lasting life. John 3:16}

It really tells us just how
much he is really into us
His only son!

Reread the Preface. Do you believe that the author accomplished her goal? Expound.

Yes, I re live some things, I've
accomplish some things. This
book has been helpful I
know I will reread again.

What can we do to show that we are into Christ?

Trust, believe, honor, praise
live and try to do Gods will
Love Him back

The Lord has promised us joy and happiness now and after death. What scriptures about life eternal do you get excited about or look forward to seeing fulfilled?

Job 23:10

Share your comments and tweets on how the chapter "He's Just That In To You" blessed you on:

https://twitter.com/StephannieBooks
http://www.blogtalkradio.com/stephanniesolomon
Facebook/Conversations With The King Ministries

Chapter Endnotes

1. Psalm 16:11 You will show me the path of life; in Your presence is fullness of joy, at Your right hand there are pleasures forevermore. (AMP)

2. Jeremiah 33:3 Call to me and I will answer you and tell you great and unsearchable things you do not know. (NIV)

3. Jeremiah 29:12 When you call on me, when you come and pray to me, I'll listen. (MSG)

4. 1 Corinthians 1:9 God, who has called you into fellowship with his Son, Jesus Christ our Lord, is faithful. (NCV)

5. Stephannie Solomon, *Living With The King :The King Our Husband,* Bloomington, Indiana, AuthorHouse, 2010, p. 10

6. Jeremiah 31:3 The LORD appeared to us in the past, saying: "I have loved you with an everlasting love; I have drawn you with unfailing kindness. (NIV)

7. Isaiah 55:3 Give ear and come to me; listen, that you may live. I will make an everlasting covenant with you, my faithful love promised to David. (NIV)

8. Romans 8:35-39 Who shall separate us from the love of Christ?... neither height nor depth, nor anything else in all creation, will be able

to separate us from the love of God that is in Christ Jesus our Lord. (NIV)

9. Philippians 1:6 God began doing a good work in you, and I am sure he will continue it until it is finished when Jesus Christ comes again. (NCV)

10. 2 Corinthians 5:8 We are confident, I say, and would prefer to be away from the body and at home with the Lord. (NIV)

11. Hebrews 13:5 Keep your lives free from the love of money, and be satisfied with what you have. God has said, "I will never leave you; I will never abandon you.(NCV)

12. 1 John 5:13 write this letter to you who believe in the Son of God so you will know you have eternal life. (NCV)

13. John 14:2 In my Father's house are many mansions: if it were not so, I would have told you. I go to prepare a place for you. (KJV)

14. James 5:10-11 Take the old prophets as your mentors. They put up with anything, went through everything, and never once quit, all the time honoring God. What a gift life is to those who stay the course! You've heard, of course, of Job's staying power, and you know how God brought it all together for him at the end. That's because God cares, cares right down to the last detail. (MSG)

15. Genesis 16:13 She gave this name to the LORD who spoke to her: "You are the God who sees

me," for she said, "I have now seen the One who sees me." (NIV)

16. Ecclesiastes 3:11 He has made everything beautiful in its time. He has also set eternity in the human heart; yet no one can fathom what God has done from beginning to end. (NIV)

17. Psalm 138:8 The Lord will perfect *that which* concerns me; Your mercy, O Lord, *endures* forever; Do not forsake the works of Your hands. (KJV)

18. Job 34:21 He has his eyes on every man and woman. He doesn't miss a trick. (MSG)

19. Hosea 14:8 Israel, have nothing to do with idols. I, the Lord, am the one who answers your prayers and watches over you. I am like a green pine tree; your blessings come from me. (NCV)

20. Zechariah 2:8 For this is what the LORD Almighty says: "After the Glorious One has sent me against the nations that have plundered you—for whoever touches you touches the apple of his eye." (NIV)

21. Genesis 6:8 But Noah found grace in the eyes of the LORD (KJV)

22. Psalm 14:2 God sticks his head out of heaven. He looks around. He's looking for someone not stupid— one man, even, God-expectant, just one God-ready woman. (MSG)

23. Psalm 33:18 Behold, the eye of the LORD is upon them that fear him, upon them that hope in his mercy;(KJV)

The Sanctified Stripper

✝

Strip yourselves of your former nature [put off and discard your old unrenewed self] which characterized your previous manner of life and becomes corrupt through lusts and desires that spring from delusion; (AMP)
Ephesians 4:22

Take It Off, Take It All Off

In 1967 a top television commercial ad for a man's shaving cream used a female model and background stripper music to get its selling point across to the viewing audience. The words of the model, "Take it off, take it all off", combined with the music became famous for its suggestiveness. That was then. Now days using implications to relay a message is nearly minimal. In this present age the envelope is pushed and an in your face approach to conveying a message is more common. Whether a woman wildly takes her clothes off in public, flashes or plays strip poker, exposing what she wears underneath is part of a multi-billion dollar industry. Stripping is seen as a worldly act centered on pleasure principles. However, stripping can be godly and centered on the Lord's principles.

Stripping for Jesus is profitable, yet not always pleasurable. Our flesh, the old nature, resists the process of becoming bare before the Lord. It would rather determine daily our wardrobe, having us wear all that is not right and unbecoming in Christ. Choosing to be led by our flesh is choosing to reject the knowledge of God. Yet bearing all to the Lord fills us with knowledge of Him and makes us new.[1] Continuing to hold onto the former way of looking at life and working out matters will eventually create a spiritual wardrobe malfunction which becomes unflattering. On the other hand, Christ our Lord desires that we be led by His Spirit.[2] Following His Spirit over our heart and mind is freeing to us. This freedom allows us to come to God naked and unashamed for He is our maker. Standing in His liberty gives Followers of Christ the confidence to see the need to strip ourselves and be renewed daily in Him.

Renewal on a daily basis requires becoming undressed before God. This starts and continues the process of godly redressing which ultimately clothes the Lord's people in His righteousness. The challenge for most women is seeing stripping as necessary. Stripping before God is good, godly, holy and highly-favored. Taking off the unrighteousness establishes inner attire that makes God's Woman a designer original; one who brings Him glory and joy. Little by little we become imitators of Christ as we take off all that does not look like Him.

Convicted

For a woman to get to the place of wanting to imitate Christ or want what He wants means that she has been convicted. Convicted is one of those multiple meaning words which can mean found or declared guilty of an offense or crime. It can also mean having an unshakable belief in something without need for proof or evidence. The latter of the two is the point of focus. To do what the Lord requires of us necessitates a relationship with Him. From this relationship comes history and knowledge of who the Lord is as well as His modus operandi.[3] He extends grace. This is an aspect of how God works. As we grow in God's grace, we will encounter several of His callings. In order to work out each calling on our life, we have to settle within the depth of who we are that God is able, will complete what He started in us and that we can do all things through Him that strengthen us.

It all boils down to moving forward as we believe the God who we cannot see. Women who live in such a way are dangerous. They intimidate those who live life pretentiously, recklessly and capriciously. Servants of God pose a serious threat to people who love 'churchin' more than living right. Choosing to live out of convictions makes one a formidable foe to false prophets, false teachers and seducers. Nonetheless, the Lord God remains faithful and will provide.[4] History with Him proves that He will not call us into anything without His grace and He does not choose us without the path and provision already set. This seems at times untrue as we confront contradictory events on the way to our purpose.

Different tactics will confront the convicted saint. By design they will be forged to convince her not to rely on her Heavenly Father for anything. She will be tempted to compromise; that is to settle for that which the Lord does not have in mind for her. Delusion and impatience will team up to persuade her that choosing what they offer will be blessed by the Lord. If the Woman of God gives in to the deceptions, she will not be comfortable. Conviction from the Holy Spirit makes her miserable because she has doubted the Lord. Regardless of the smiles, justification, make up and cohorts who agree with the sin, if you are really God's Woman, you are continually uncomfortable with being out of line with Christ. We can fake contentment, but our actions will confirm that conviction and compromise cannot dwell happily together. Conviction is of the Light and compromise is from the dark. Light and darkness have no fellowship.[5] God is Light and there is no darkness in Him.[6] Ladies, the Lord will not bless sin no matter how we and others attempt to justify it.

Moreover, finding someone to cosign our sin is not pleasing to the Lord either.[7] Looking for partners in crime only adds another soul to whom we are accountable to as a partaker in unrighteousness. If the crew, click or girlfriends of choice condone that which is unholy, consistently put the cart before the horse, partake in the same kind of dismal indiscretions or work to make others feel comfortable with sin, then we are not being challenged to be the best in Christ. This is also evidence that we may need a new group to encircle us. Challenge yourself and grow dear sister. Affiliate with sisters who have stepped up their game in Christ. Because of Him, they have changed the game, the way society and sub-cultures see life. They have become game changers (See pgs. 20-22). This message is not meant to condemn, for there is no condemnation to those who are in Christ Jesus.[8] Being convicted and condemned are not the same. Just as conviction and compromise are not cut from the same cloth, neither are conviction and condemnation of the same mold. Christ came that we would not be condemned or live a life of conformity and compromise. We get convicted by His Holy Spirit to live right in Him when we miss the mark or sin. Since we are born of God we should be uncomfortable with doing wrong. We are the righteousness of God. Wrongdoing is sin and there is no sin in Christ Jesus. We should not want to continue in it.[9] In introspect and retrospect it's simply a matter of the Christian hating what God hates and loving what He loves.

So many things can be a porthole for the enemies of Christ to work through. One's health, employment, finances, marriage, family, children, and faith are all up for grabs. There is no holds bar in the attack which is designed to take Women of Faith off of God's stage. Like the Lord's servant Job, everything except our life may be permitted to be touched. The craftiness of the prince of the power of the air is not always deterred by this. If one's godly witness is blemished and causes individuals to doubt the power of Christ, this ofttimes is good enough for Satan.

In all, there is so much beauty that comes out of the woman who is convicted to grow in God's grace. His favor flows with the woman who chooses to live out her convictions. Not that we live for the approval of people, but in time there will be those who see the hand of God actively leading and providing for women living with unshakable faith. Time will tell all. Patience is key.[10] Rushing one's personal and unique process does not lead to victory. In addition, comparing one's process to someone else's experience is not wise because what the Lord has ordained for each woman is for her and no one else. One woman's prime may differ from another woman' time of vigor and success, but what the Lord has promised will come to pass. The Living Word states in Psalm 31:15 that our times are in His hands, not in the hands of the world or even ourselves. Therefore, praying and fasting about the things needed to endure until the appointed time should be in effect. At the right time we all should want to get our blessings when the Lord says that its time.

Conviction is a layer of spiritual clothing that Women of Faith must drape themselves in. It compliments any outfit. It is grace's way of leading us into the new person who Christ wants us to experience.

Covered

When women and girls strip their former nature and allow the Lord to clothe them in His righteousness, humility overtakes them[11]. They do not have to say that they are humbled, they just are. Being humble speaks for them. Clothed in humility and other virtues, they showcase the righteousness of God. I regard such females as covered girls and covered women. These female disciples have the assurance that Jesus has their best interest. Their lives are not shaped by things or feelings. Instead, they are shaped by the Living God who has not and will never leave them comfortless, empty and naked. He consoles, consumes and clothes them in His holiness. Moreover, He equips them with the spirit of wisdom and revelation.[12] Thus, as they strip from envy, slander, gossip, malice, a foul mouth, fornication, low self-esteem, adultery, covetousness, debauchery, idolatry, selfishness, lying, manipulation, and other evidences of an impure heart, the Lord raises Himself in them. He leads them to a revived and revised life of holiness which reflects God within.

Covered girls are not too young to strip for Jesus and covered women are not too old to undress and expose themselves before their Maker and Master. Humility has made them aware that their strength and sufficiency do not come from them, but all of their help and resources come from the Lord. Yet, such highly favored worshippers are not solely identified by the presence of humility. Living with their imperfections, they continue living to imitate God. They are h oly as He is holy. They prove their love for the Lord by obeying all of his commandments.[13] As they undress unrighteousness and remove the bad attitude, self-loathing, aggrandizement, jealousy, self-intoxication, and other vices, the world sees women who are a class act, authentic game changers because they are allowing Christ to make them over.

In the early 1960's the legendary singer Dionne Warwick sang a song written by Burt Bacharach and Hal David entitled, "Don't Make Me Over". Even now I can hear it playing from the stereo in our living room. My mother and stepfather were fans of this singer, so whatever songs they purchased and listened to, I heard and learned. This song was one of many that I liked and sang. It became a hit. The world seemed to love the tune and lyrics. The world also witnessed a makeover from the one singing the hit song. Dionne Warwick evolved not only to become a top and leading singer for years, but she evolved to become one of the most striking & best dressed ladies of the time. The lyrics of this song stressed being accepted for what one does and who one is. A reality for many of us is that we want to be embraced for who we are and what we do. However, it is in Christ where we find out who we are and who He wants us to become. Christ accepts us while desiring that we permit Him to make us over, totally. Unlike the world's view of a total makeover that is superficial and starts with the exterior of a person, for the Children of God and Women of Worth renewal is from the inside out. Confidence is not meant to come from a change in hair color, cut and style. Esteem building is not designed to spring forth via loss of weight, a fresh relationship with a man or other ways that societies endorse. We are called to yield to the power of Christ's Holy Spirit that raised Him from the grave and is alive in us; believers of this truth. A makeover in Christ Jesus the Lord covers the gamut of who we are; thus, making us healed and whole persons. No aspect of our being or our personhood is off limits to being made anew in Him.

Living covered in Christ affords us so much. Understand that being made over never means that Christ will cover all of our ills. There are seasons in life where He keeps our dirty laundry from human view with a desire that we entrust our mess to Him. He will cover it and us with His Grace and His Blood. The Blood that Christ shed for the world is so powerful that it can and will cleanse, cover and convert our sin sick souls. It is up to us to take advantage of the opportunities of His grace by way of prayer, confession, repentance and living out His words. Applying these principles allows Him to make us over. Having our nature be made new in Christ is important. Only Christ is the author and engineer of an authentic new nature. He knows the new you and the new me that has been resolved beforehand. Moreover, He is the paradigm for us to follow and emulate in our newness.[14] In Him disciples live, move and have their being, for it is in trusting in Him that we are saved, healed and delivered. Truly, aging covered by the hand of God has so many benefits.

When Christ is at the forefront of what we do, many negative labels, stereotypes and perceptions will be stripped from us. Rather than being known as "a piece of work", many of the Lord's followers will be called "God's handiwork". His covering will not always prevent every anti-God, anti-you spirit from attacking, but it will cause people to take a second look at the beauty of the Lord that overtakes His covered vessels. People will do a double take at the results of God's covering. Some may never admit the glorious change, but they will take notice of our godly makeover. Our significance which had not been completely grasped at first will capture attention and surprise many.

A godly makeover strips us of pride, deception, impenitence, hate, defiance, folly, rebellion and much more so that we are clothed in humility, purity, integrity, repentance, love, obedience, wisdom, submission and every godly attribute of Christ Jesus. The makeover, covering, conviction and stripping are all essential aspects of our evolution in Christ. Each evidences the grace of God that is active and abounds through the years. The matchless work of grace transforms the female heart, mind and spirit. God's grace has been granted for us to think and behave like His son.[15] Therefore, no longer does dysfunctions and disaster have power over us. They may confront, but they cannot conquer when grace has its perfect work in us. God's grace will refine the rough, crude, homely, impulsive, woman into one who elegantly endures her personal trials. Her suffering will look easy to outsiders. Because of grace, everything that she does in and for Christ is superior; above the norm. She is set apart, radiating so much differently than the rest.

Every woman and girl who acknowledges and appreciates the grace of God walks in His authority. One way that she exemplifies use of her God given authority is by having command of her time and her thoughts. A faithful woman is obligated to her total wellness, family, profession, church, and social organization. In essence each of these ought to be a blessing. Yet, having to meet multiple demands simultaneously can be physically, emotionally, mentally and spiritually draining. The covered woman will glorify her Heavenly Father by learning to say "no" to some requests and demands of life. Without guilt, she gracefully declines and denounces "tyranny of the urgent" and the busy-ness of life. Oftentimes, when people see our faithfulness to things entrusted to us, they imagine us assisting them in areas that require faithfulness.[16] Where people see us is not always where the Lord sees us or plants us. It is essential for good health and wholeness to retreat, step back and assess, reflect, evaluate and then proceed forward in Christ our Lord. Herein one takes ownership or command of one's time. This must happen; otherwise, we may find ourselves being heavenly minded doing no earthly good. An aspect of spiritual growth is not finding everything utterly important at the moment in which it is presented. Also, a mature servant discerns what the Lord would have her to do and where she ought to be working for the Lord and how long. Being stripped of her former self, she rests in the ways of Christ, not others.

We have to seize the day by doing what we are called by the Lord to do in the time that He has given us.[17] There will be distractions and things that are important as well as matters that should be addressed with urgency will arise.[18] However, the Lord will give each of us a plan that prioritizes the events of our day and our life. Disapprovals of the Lord's way will develop, but stick with His plan. Come what may, stay the course.[19] People will leave and disagree with us. Some will threaten to detach themselves from us and the mission we are sanctioned to accomplish, taking their resources with them. Still the covering of the Lord will sustain us. In cases like this, know dear sister that the Lord will give you a strategy to show you who is really with you and who believes that the Lord is using you for Kingdom service. True lovers of God will find ways to truly support the work and worth of God at work in you.

Remember covered girls and women are kept girls and kept women. Let opponents do what they do. Even when forgiving them of wrong doings, know that we do not need them. We need Christ. This is hard to receive for some for many believe that we need people who do not have our best interest. Yet, there are people who understand "tough love" and what it means to love at a distance because the dysfunction and rebellion coming from a loved one is a kill joy. Carriers of a kill joy spirit can consist of spouses, children, parents, siblings, members of a team, church, etc. We do not want to believe that we have to walk away from or allow them to walk away from us. There are times when distance is necessary. Stand your ground, fighting the good fight of faith as the Lord leads. Love them as the Lord leads, but discern when you are giving your pearls to swine.[20] A good Christian woman will forgive others of their trespasses, but know that you do not need people who disrespect and try to smother your anointing.

There is comfort in being covered by the Lord. Authority to walk and freedom to live like never before is afforded to those who have taken off the old and put on the new. This is the life of a sanctified stripper. Even after she overcomes an aspect of her life tainted with dysfunction, she strips another layer of self away so that Christ is always glorified in her.[21] She is learning as she grows. The ongoing process of conviction and stripping creates a woman who wins in Christ, a super role model, a big girl in Jesus and a sanctified stripper. Regardless of age, the grace of God allows girls and women to grow daily into the image that He created. Aging with grace is wonder filled and a learning process. Growing older is natural and should not be feared, but embraced with the grace of God that comes at any age.

Reflection

Prayer: Lord Jesus Ephesians 4:22 is a powerful scripture. Where should I begin stripping so that I begin to look more like you?

Stop fornicating.

Oftentimes we do not realize what in our life has to go, be removed because it has been around so long and/or it defines our past, family and environment. List at least two things in your life that need to be stripped.

Certain men

Are you afraid to remove them? Is there resistance in stripping? Explain.

I want so bad them to be removed. so bad that it frustrates me. I'm not afraid to let it go its that they won't go and I hit back doors with another.

Conviction and guilt are often grouped together or used synonymously. What is the difference between these two words?

I convict myself because I believe I can strip these things but then I feel guilty for some very odd reason

Worldly strippers ultimately work to get people excited about taking clothes off. What should sanctified strippers be excited about and work to get others excited about?

Removing that fake and phony cover and let the true God fearing person show. When you ushered about Christ and then yourself if no one else get excited you still will.

How does the foundational scripture relate to this chapter?

[Strip yourselves of your former nature [put off and discard your old unrenewed self] which characterized your previous manner of life and becomes corrupt through lusts and desires that spring from delusion; Ephesians 4:22]

TAKE IT OFF !!!

Share your comments and tweets on how the chapter "The Sanctified Stripper" blessed you on:

https://twitter.com/StephannieBooks
http://www.blogtalkradio.com/stephanniesolomon
Facebook/Conversations With The King Ministries

Chapter Endnotes

1. Colossians 3:10 You have begun to live the new life, in which you are being made new and are becoming like the One who made you. This new life brings you the true knowledge of God. (NCV)

2. Galatians 5:18 But if you are led by the Spirit, you are not under the law. (NIV)

3. Stephannie Solomon. *Living With The King: God's Modus Operandi.* Bloomongton, Indiana, AuthorHouse, 2010, p. 4-6.

4. Genesis 22:14 So Abraham called the name of that place The Lord Will Provide. And it is said to this day, On the mount of the Lord it will be provided. (AMP)

5. 2 Corinthians 6:14 *Warning About Non-Christians*] You are not the same as those who do not believe. So do not join yourselves to them. Good and bad do not belong together. Light and darkness cannot share together. (NCV)

6. 1 John 1:5 [*Light and Darkness, Sin and Forgiveness*] This is the message we have heard from him and declare to you: God is light; in him there is no darkness at all. (NIV)

7. Ephesians 5:7 Therefore do not be partakers with them. (KJV)

8. Romans 8:1 There is therefore now no condemnation to those who are in Christ Jesus, who do not walk according to the flesh, but according to the Spirit. (KJV)

9. 1 John 5:17-18 Doing wrong is always sin, but there is sin that does not lead to eternal death. We know that those who are God's children do not continue to sin. The Son of God keeps them safe, and the Evil One cannot touch them. (NCV)

10. Luke 21:19 By your patience possess your souls. (KJV)

11. 1 Peter 5:5 Likewise, you who are younger and of lesser rank, be subject to the elders (the ministers and spiritual guides of the church)—[giving them due respect and yielding to their counsel]. Clothe (apron) yourselves, all of you, with humility [as the garb of a servant, so that its covering cannot possibly be stripped from you, with freedom from pride and arrogance] toward one another. For God sets Himself against the proud (the insolent, the overbearing, the disdainful, the presumptuous, the boastful)—[and He opposes, frustrates, and defeats them], but gives grace (favor, blessing) to the humble. (AMP)

12. Ephesians 1:17 I keep asking that the God of our Lord Jesus Christ, the glorious Father, may give you the Spirit of wisdom and revelation, so that you may know him better. (NIV)

13. John 14:15 If you love me, you will obey my commands. (NCV)

14. Carl J. Solomon, "It's All Because Of Christ," sermon preached at the United Baptist Church, Baltimore, Maryland, 2 September 2012.

15. Philippians 2:5 Let this mind be in you, which was also in Christ Jesus: (KJV)

16. Luke 12:48 But he who did not know and did things worthy of a beating shall be beaten with few [lashes]. For everyone to whom much is given, of him shall much be required; and of him to whom men entrust much, they will require and demand all the more. (AMP)

17. Luke 19:13 And he called his ten servants, and delivered them ten pounds, and said unto them, Occupy till I come. (KJV)

18. Charles Hummel," Tyranny of the Urgent", *Intervarsity Christian Fellowship.* 1967.

19. Stephannie Solomon, *Living With The King: Stay The Course.* Bloomington, Indiana, AuthorHouse, 2010,pp. 135-138.

20. Matthew 7:6 Give not that which is holy unto the dogs, neither cast ye your pearls before swine, lest they trample them under their feet, and turn again and rend you. (KJV)

21. 2 Thessalonians 1:12 Thus may the name of our Lord Jesus Christ be glorified and become more glorious through and in you, and may you [also be glorified] in Him according to the grace (favor and blessing) of our God and the Lord Jesus Christ (the Messiah, the Anointed One). (AMP)

About the Author

Stephannie E. R. Solomon is an accomplished Christian author who writes with a disciple-centric flare. Her reliance on biblical principles, use of the conversational style, passion for teaching, willingness to share from her well of wisdom help to characterize her style as an expositor and writer. She teaches through her books on Blog Talk Radio and for the past 15 years has been a sought out facilitator, presenter and speaker for Christian and non-Christian events. Responsive readers of her books and blogs, as well as loyal listeners of her web radio broadcast, look forward to her annual disciple-centric retreats. Mrs. Solomon is also the solo author of Conversations With The King and Living With The King. She is a contributing author of Sister Strength and Sister To Sister: Devotions For and From African American Women.

Being a wife, mother and educator are other areas in which this author seeks to serve the Lord in grace and excellence.